WOULD YOU EAT YOUR CAT?

Published in 2010 by New Holland Publishers (UK) Ltd
London · Cape Town · Sydney · Auckland
www.newhollandpublishers.com

Garfield House, 86-88 Edgware Road,
London W2 2EA, United Kingdom

10 9 8 7 6 5 4 3 2 1

Conceived and produced by
Elwin Street Limited
144 Liverpool Road
London N1 1LA
www.elwinstreet.com

A catalogue record for this book is available from the
British Library.

ISBN 978 1 84773 668 0

Designed by: Amanda Jekums

Printed and bound in China

WOULD YOU EAT YOUR CAT?

KEY ETHICAL CONUNDRUMS

AND WHAT THEY TELL YOU ABOUT YOURSELF

JEREMY STANGROOM

NH

NEW
HOLLAND

Contents

Introduction 6

CRIME AND PUNISHMENT 36

Thought experiments to illuminate issues of personal responsibility, culpability and punishment

SOCIETY AND POLITICS 50

How is moral reasoning affected by the fact that we live in a world of nation states and fellow citizens?

RESPONSES 66

Discover the philosophical background to each conundrum and what your responses say about you

INTRODUCTION

You had been happily married for 14 years when it happened – your head was turned by a hot young thing you met on Facebook. Well, at least you thought you'd met a hot young thing, but when you met for what you hoped would be a clandestine affair of the flesh, your date turned out to be a surprisingly unattractive trucker from Wigan.

Chastened, you rushed back home, only to find that your spouse had been through your email. Happily there was nothing there too incriminating. Unhappily you are now troubled by a guilty conscience, and your spouse is getting suspicious. Should you confess all?

Part of the interest of a moral dilemma such as this one, and the others like it featured in this book is that how we deal with it tells us something about our general approach to morality.

Utilitarianism

Perhaps, for example, you think that the key issue here is whether or not you will make the world a happier place by confessing to your spouse. If so, then your moral approach is utilitarian – that is, it is in accordance with the idea that the moral worth of an act is determined by how it contributes to the balance between happiness and unhappiness aggregated across everybody.

This might sound a little complex, but it is summed up succinctly by the phrase: 'the greatest good for the greatest number of people'. So if confessing to your spouse results in more total happiness – or good – than not confessing, then it is right to confess.

Utilitarianism has its origins in the work of the 18th-century philosopher Jeremy Bentham. He noted that people tend to act in their own interests, which mainly involves pursuing pleasure and attempting to minimize pain. Individual human happiness, therefore, consists in making sure that you have more pleasure than pain; which in turn means that in order to maximize human happiness overall, you have to achieve as great a balance of pleasure over pain as possible for the greatest number of people. This is Bentham's 'Greatest Happiness Principle'. So in determining how we should act, we must:

> Sum up all the values of all the pleasures on the one side, and those of all the pains on the other. The balance, if it be on the side of pleasure, will give the good tendency of the act upon the whole...

This focus on the effects of an action means that utilitarianism is a consequentialist theory: the worth of an action is determined by its outcomes.

Deontological Ethics

Although consequentialism is highly influential in the world of ethical philosophy, it is not the only way to approach moral issues. Thus, for example, it is possible you think that it would be wrong to lie to your spouse about your encounter with the trucker, regardless of the consequences. Lying is just wrong. If so, then it is likely you'll have some sympathy with what are called deontological approaches to morality.

Deontological ethics, in contrast to the various stripes of consequentialism, holds that actions are not justified by their effects, but by whether or not they are in accordance with a moral norm. In other words, deontology holds that actions are intrinsically good or bad, regardless of their consequences: a moral agent is duty bound to obey what is right, even if it is at the cost of some terrible outcome.

Immanuel Kant is perhaps the most important philosopher to have espoused a deontological moral philosophy. For Kant, acting morally is not a matter of assessing consequences, but of acting out of respect for the moral law. The moral law has a categorical form: 'Do this' or 'Don't do that'. Therefore, if lying or deception is prohibited, as Kant believed them to be, it would be wrong not to confess to your spouse, even if the consequences of confessing were disastrous.

Virtue Ethics
A third way of thinking through moral issues stresses the cultivation of character or virtue. The virtue ethics approach is rooted in ancient Greek philosophy, and particularly the ideas of Aristotle, who thought that virtue consists in acting in accordance with reason by always choosing the mean between the extremes of excess and deficiency. The moral virtues that Aristotle identified in this fashion included justice, fortitude, courage, temperance and prudence.

Virtue ethics does not provide a rule book for action in the same way as some other moral frameworks, but it is far from empty in terms of what it tells us about how we should behave. People should act in a way that is most likely to contribute to the cultivation of a virtuous character. A virtue ethicist will not necessarily conclude that you're behaving badly if you deceive your spouse on this particular occasion; however, if you consistently deceive him or her, across a range of issues, then Aristotle certainly, and likely other virtue ethicists, would conclude that your behaviour was wrong.

There are no easy answers to the issues raised by the moral conundrums and dilemmas featured in this book. In a sense, this is the whole point: by raising difficult questions it shows us how we tend to think about ethics and the like. As you work through the book, you will find things out about philosophy, ethics, your philosophical world view and yourself. No doubt you'll be infuriated at times, and discombobulated at others, but above all the hope is that you'll enjoy yourself and be stimulated by the journey.

HOW TO USE THIS BOOK

This book features 25 ethical conundrums that are designed to illuminate various issues in moral philosophy, and at the same time shed some light on your own moral commitments. The conundrums are set up in the first half of the book, and each is associated with a particular moral question, which you should attempt to answer. The second half of the book features an analysis of each conundrum, which discusses the philosophical background of the issue under consideration, possible solutions to the question posed and some of the implications of those solutions.

The best way to read this book is conundrum by conundrum; read one, think about the issues involved, attempt to answer the question and then turn to the back of the book to see how your answer stacks up against the philosophical and ethical issues raised. You will also find a morality barometer associated with each conundrum, which will tell you a little bit about what your response indicates about your own moral framework.

Moral conundrums that have perplexed
some of the greatest philosophical minds

1

ETHICAL IMPASSES

Would You Eat Your Cat?
Is It Always Ok To Look At Your Own Photos?
Is It Better To Be A Sexist Than A Misanthrope?
Are We Morally Obliged To End The World?
Are We Really Sorry That Hitler Existed?
Should We Sacrifice One To Save Five?

We like to think that moral questions have clear answers. It is true that we will probably accept that different people will come up with different answers, but many of us will be discomforted by the idea that some moral questions have no obvious answers at all.

In the normal course of events, this circumstance will not occur. We might not agree about whether abortion is moral, for example, but at least we know how to go about assessing the case. However, there is a set of moral conundrums where it is not clear how we should even get started thinking about the issues involved: the more we examine their various moral complexities, the more we hold these up against our moral intuitions, the more confused we become.

Welcome to the world of pets for dinner, runaway trains and demagogues who want to end the world.

WOULD YOU EAT YOUR CAT?

Cleo Patrick had always enjoyed a close relationship with her cat, Hector. She would tell her friends that she and Hector were more like sister and brother than owner and pet. Hector went everywhere with Cleo. He would ride in the trolley as she stocked up on his favourite gourmet foods at her weekly supermarket shop. They would regularly watch afternoon reruns of *Melrose Place* together, she enjoying the occasional After Eight mint, he happily devouring a tuna melt. And at night he would curl up at the bottom of her bed and she would read to him – an Agatha Christie, perhaps, or excerpts from *The Owl and the Pussycat*.

Hector, unfortunately, was not blessed with great eyesight and this led to his downfall, when one day he mistook a lawnmower for a mouse. Cleo was devastated by his death. But having known that this moment would come, she had, some years before, made herself a promise: as a tribute to Hector, she would eat him for supper. She felt that this was fitting – he

would in death become one with her. Also, she had heard that cat meat was jolly tasty and she figured that Hector would have been pleased that he was now satisfying her curiosity in this regard.

So it was, then, that Cleo sat down on the evening of Hector's death and ate him on toast, washed down with a nice glass of Chianti. Cleo lived to be a ripe old age. She never regretted her decision to eat Hector, never suffered any ill-effects as a result and told nobody else what she had done.

*Was Cleo wrong to eat her beloved cat
as if he were just a bedtime snack?*

RESPONSE ON PAGE 68

IS IT ALWAYS OK TO LOOK AT YOUR OWN PHOTOS?

Venus Titian was 18 when she allowed her then boyfriend, Milo Reuben, to take photographs of her naked. Her decision was not coerced in any way, and the photographs were artistic in style rather than pornographic. A few years later, Venus and Milo split up, and Milo offered to destroy the photographs. Venus said that she was happy for him to keep them on condition that he never showed them to anybody else. He agreed, and they went their separate ways.

Twenty years later, Venus is now a minor celebrity, about to appear on sheep-pursuit reality show, *I'm a Celebrity Shepherd*. Milo still has the photographs, but has started to worry that perhaps there is some moral wrong in his looking at them. He would never show them to anybody else, and has no particular reason to think that the celebrity Venus would object (though given her public profile he knows that this is a possibility). Nevertheless, he still wonders whether he ought to destroy them. He can't help but think that it might be immoral for a man in his forties to be looking at naked photos of an ex-girlfriend that were taken 20 years previously when she was only 18.

Is Milo wrong to look at the photographs?

RESPONSE ON PAGE 71

Quick Dilemma

Two sailors are shipwrecked, and end up in the water, swimming for their lives. They spot a plank of wood, and both swim towards it. Unfortunately, the plank will only support one of them. Sailor A arrives at the plank first. This means Sailor B is doomed to drown. However, rather than accepting his fate, Sailor B shoves Sailor A off the plank, and then paddles away at high speed. As a result, Sailor A, rather than Sailor B, drowns. Sailor B is eventually rescued, but there is no doubt he would have drowned had he not pushed Sailor A off the plank. At any subsequent murder trial, can Sailor B claim that he acted in self-defence?

Quick Dilemma

You're a fan of Manchester City football club. You loathe your local rival Manchester United with the heat of a fiery nova. After United lose the Champions League final to Barcelona, you find yourself glorying in the misery of the United fans. It's *schadenfreude* run riot. But then it occurs to you that there is something a little bit odd about your reaction. You are pleased that the United fans are miserable, and yet they haven't done anything wrong, nothing to deserve their misery, except support a football team that happens to be the local rival of the team that you support. How is it possible to justify your reaction?

IS IT BETTER TO BE A SEXIST THAN A MISANTHROPE?

Harold Carpenter and Lou Bishop are neighbours in sun-kissed Erinsford, a town nestled on the Humberside Riviera. Harold, unfortunately, does not share the sunny disposition of his home town. He's a misanthrope. He dislikes people – a lot. He doesn't have friends, and he views his acquaintances with barely concealed contempt. Harold is very much an equal opportunity misanthrope – he dislikes men, women, straights, gays, blacks, whites and one-legged people all with an equal intensity. To his credit, he is aware that his misanthropy is a problem, so he keeps to himself as much as possible. Nevertheless, he is certainly a negative force in the world, subtracting from rather than adding to the sum total of human happiness.

Lou Bishop is a different kettle of fish altogether. He *likes* most people a lot. He considers even his neighbours to be good friends, and treats *nearly* everybody he meets with consideration and kindness. However, he is an unreconstructed male chauvinist. He believes that men are intellectually superior to women, and thinks that the 'fairer sex' are really only suited to be homemakers. He cannot cope with 'modern' women at all: as far as he is concerned, women should be kept as far away as possible from manly pursuits such as making money

and playing golf. Lou is aware that society frowns upon his sexism, so he tries to avoid modern women as much as he can. Nevertheless, in his dealings with them, he is definitely a negative force in the world, subtracting from rather than adding to the sum total of human happiness.

FURTHER FACTS ABOUT HAROLD AND LOU:

1. Harold treats 'modern' women worse than Lou treats them. Not because he's a sexist – he isn't – just because he doesn't like people.
2. Lou treats everybody better than Harold treats anybody.
3. Harold *does not* discriminate whereas Lou does. Harold would employ a woman to do a job if she was the best candidate. Lou would not.

Which is worse,
Harold's misanthropy or Lou's sexism?

RESPONSE ON PAGE 74

ARE WE MORALLY OBLIGED TO END THE WORLD?

Roger Dalton is one of a new breed of secret agents. Thoroughly schooled in Gestalt therapy, counselling and neuro-linguistic programming, he has given up his licence to kill for a licence to sit and chat with his enemies in order to show them the errors of their ways. This is not turning out to be an easy option. Evil geniuses really can be very stubborn. Often they seem quite convinced that their evil is justified.

Dalton is having particular trouble with a John 'Goldtooth' Bentham. Goldtooth seems convinced that his plan to vaporize the entire world is morally justified. He argues as follows:

We have a strong moral duty to minimize suffering. This trumps any duty that we might have to maximize happiness. Unfortunately, most people on earth spend a lot of their time suffering. Death, disease, hunger and pain are our constant companions. We don't do so badly in the West, albeit we're hardly free from suffering, but other people are not so lucky. Life is a vale of tears, characterized by our sighs, mourning and weeping.

In contrast, non-existence is an entirely unproblematic state.
Nobody suffers before they are born, and the number of people
who are perturbed by the thought that they did not exist before their
birth is vanishingly small.

It follows, then, that non-existence is preferable to existence if one
wants to minimize suffering. If nobody exists then there is no suffering.
Therefore, or at least so Goldtooth argues, there is a moral requirement
to bring an end to human existence. Vaporizing the world is a duty.

Roger Dalton is reluctant to think that there is anything to this argument. Yet he can't quite see where it goes wrong. He realises that if Goldtooth makes good on his intention to vaporize the Earth, it will interfere with a lot of people's plans for the evening, but he's not sure that Goldtooth will be persuaded that this is a reason for abandoning his dastardly scheme. It is not entirely clear how Dalton should counter Goldtooth's argument.

Is Goldtooth right that we should end the world?

RESPONSE ON PAGE 77

ARE WE REALLY SORRY THAT HITLER EXISTED?

Claire Henri is the wife of a professional time traveller. Unfortunately, as far as she can tell, he isn't much good at his job. The usual pattern of events sees him hopping into his time machine, disappearing and then reappearing a few seconds later, often naked and muttering something about Warlocks.

She is determined that he should show more ambition in his time-travelling exploits. It is clear that he needs structure and a plan. So with no thought of the perils of science fiction cliché, she suggests that he goes back in time to kill Hitler.

Her husband does not greet this plan with much enthusiasm. Although he is tempted to lecture her on the dangers of creating a rupture in the space-time continuum, he takes a different tack.

TIME TRAVELLER: *Surely my dear, you cannot be sorry that Hitler existed?*

CLAIRE: *What do you mean?! Hitler was a monster! Of course I'm sorry he existed!*

TIME TRAVELLER: *Yes, but if he had not existed, then your parents would never have met during that air raid, and you would not have been born. Are you sorry that you were born? If you are not, then it does not make sense to say that you are sorry that Hitler existed.*

CLAIRE: *You've been spending too much time with those Warlocks, Mister! I tell you I am sorry Hitler was born. I feel very sorry for all his victims.*

TIME TRAVELLER: *Ah yes, but there's a difference between feeling sorry for people and empathizing with their suffering, and being* sorry that something occurred. Your plan is that I should go back in time to kill Hitler. I put it to you that you don't really mean what you say. You are not sorry you were born, which means that you cannot be sorry that Hitler existed, even if you do feel empathy for his victims.

CLAIRE: But wouldn't that make me rather immoral? Surely we're morally required to be sorry that things as horrible as the consequences of Hitler's birth occurred?

TIME TRAVELLER: Ah well, it seems we have a moral paradox; which reminds me, did I ever tell you about that time I was sucked into a wormhole…

CLAIRE: Yes dear, now what time did you say you were meeting those Warlocks?

Is the Time Traveller right?
If your existence depends on some large harm, and you do not regret your existence, does that mean that you cannot be sorry that the large harm occurred?

RESPONSE ON PAGE 80

ETHICAL IMPASSES   21

SHOULD WE SACRIFICE ONE
TO SAVE FIVE?

Pacey Bones, train driver extraordinaire, is facing something of a dilemma. He has just been informed that an unfortunate design fault in his locomotive, *The Speedy Bullock*, means that if its speed drops below 50 mph before it reaches the next station, it will explode, killing all 500 passengers on board the carriages it is pulling. This would be bad enough, but he has also been told that there are five people tied to the track between it and the next station. The good news is that Pacey can press a button, which will temporarily divert the train into a siding, allowing it to pass harmlessly by the five people tied to the track. The bad news is that if he does, the train will run over a person who has become attached to the siding track as a result of a stag night jape involving a tube of superglue.

If he presses the button, the man glued to the siding track will die. If he doesn't press the button, the five people tied to the track the train is already travelling along will die. There is no way that nobody will die.

Should Pacey press the button?

RESPONSE ON PAGE 83

?

Quick Dilemma

The date is 2150, and the Earth has been devastated as a result of our mistreatment of the environment. Because of the toxicity of the Earth's atmosphere, great numbers of people are being born with horrible physical problems, and are condemned to live out lives that are painful and short. However, if the Earth had not been systematically mistreated, then these people would not have been born at all (since the past and present would be entirely different). Are they in a position to complain about what has happened to the Earth (given that it is a condition of their existence)?

?

Quick Dilemma

You are one of the world's leading experts on antique glass swans. While holidaying in Morecambe, you find a very valuable Napoleonic era swan in a junk shop for £4.37. You rush to the counter to buy it, only to find that the shop owner looks like your mother. Suddenly you have moral qualms. How can it be okay to take advantage of this woman's lack of knowledge, and deprive her of what would be a large sum of money if she were to sell the item at auction? Isn't this just a legal version of swiping £10,000 that you find hidden in somebody's house, and saying, 'Ah well, they didn't know it was there…'?

How free should we be to behave as we wish?

RIGHTS AND RESPONSIBILITIES

Should Climbing Mountains Be Banned?
Should We Have Sex When Drunk?
Can I Bring Poison Onto A Bus?
Whose Body Is It Anyway?
Is It Wrong To Commit Suicide?

The proper limits of personal freedom is an issue that has been debated almost since people began debating things at all and which remains a central area of contention today.

Are we free to criticize other people's sacred beliefs? Should assisted suicide be legal? Are we at liberty to view pictures of sadomasochistic sexual activity? Should we be allowed to use our mobile phones while driving?

These issues have all been in the headlines recently. But there is no consensus about how we should view them. This is partly because people come to them from different political and ethical traditions: a liberal person just isn't going to think about assisted suicide, for example, in the same way as a conservative. But it is also because there are genuine and deep moral complexities involved in thinking about the proper limits of personal freedom. The various scenarios featured in this section will illustrate some of this complexity.

SHOULD CLIMBING MOUNTAINS BE BANNED?

POLICEMAN: *Sorry sir, you can't go up there!*

CLIMBER: *What do you mean?! It's Ben Nevis. I want to climb Ben Nevis!*

POLICEMAN: *Too dangerous.*

CLIMBER: *Too dangerous?*

POLICEMAN: *Yes sir. People die every year on Ben Nevis. It's not safe.*

CLIMBER: *But you can't stop people doing things just because they're dangerous. That's absurd!*

POLICEMAN: *There's nothing absurd about it. Take prescription drugs, for example. You can't just buy them over the counter, now, can you? And for good reason: they're not safe. You might overdose, or become addicted, or self-medicate. We restrict access to drugs in order to keep the public safe. It's the same with Ben Nevis. If you don't have a pass, you're not going up.*

CLIMBER: *But surely it's up to me whether I put my life in danger?*

POLICEMAN: *Not always, sir, no. We're not just going to let you commit suicide, are we? Also did you know that if two doctors decide that you have a mental illness, we can lock you up if we think you're a danger to yourself?*

CLIMBER: *Hey, come on! Those are both extreme cases. Normally we're allowed to put our lives at least a little bit at risk.*

POLICEMAN: *Again, I say to you, not always, sir. Consider Class A drugs. Part of the reason they're illegal is that they are dangerous for the people who use them. Heroin, for example, carries the risk of death from accidental overdose and addiction. Would you want to spend your life chasing your next fix? No you wouldn't. That's why it's illegal.*

CLIMBER: *That's certainly not the only reason it's illegal! Drug use has social costs. That's a big part of the reason drugs are illegal.*

POLICEMAN: *Climbing Ben Nevis has social costs. Have you any idea how often we have had to call out the Mountain Rescue team to fetch some stranded climber off the slopes?*

CLIMBER: *Well what about walking a tightrope? Or the Isle of Man TT race? Should they be banned?*

POLICEMAN: *Quite possibly, sir.*

CLIMBER: *OK, so what about driving a car? In the UK, more than 3,000 people die every year in road traffic accidents, and there are huge social costs associated with driving. So are you going to make driving illegal?*

POLICEMAN: *Sir, the fact that you know how many people die every year in road accidents is troubling and perplexing. As to your question, well, I'll leave that to greater intellects than my own.*

So is the policeman right?
Should people be banned from doing
dangerous things such as climbing mountains?

RESPONSE ON PAGE 85

SHOULD WE HAVE SEX WHEN DRUNK?

Dido and Aeneas, first year students of philosophy and husbandry, have become inseparable during Fresher's week at Carthage University. However, as they are somewhat conservative in their attitudes towards love, they have not yet consummated their dalliance. This situation, however, is under threat after they spend an evening quaffing wine under the cypress trees at their halls of residence.

AENEAS: *Your golden locks are more resplendent than the most resplendent of sunsets, my darling. Thou art more lovely and more…*

DIDO: *Yeah, what are you after, Aeneas?*

AENEAS: *Well, I think it might be time to express our love in a more physical manner — a union of body and soul.*

DIDO: *You want sex?*

AENEAS: *Pretty much, yes.*

DIDO: *I'm tempted, but it'll probably end badly. For all I know you might run off to Italy afterwards…*

AENEAS: *Never, my love. I am yours until Aphrodite herself rips out my heart.*

DIDO: *I doubt that, Aeneas, but anyway there's another issue here. We've been drinking. We can't be sure that we really want to have sex. We might be taking advantage of each other…*

AENEAS: *Come on Dido, that's setting the bar for consent way too high. People often regret sexual encounters: the fact that tomorrow we might wish we hadn't had sex, doesn't mean we that we don't want to have it now.*

DIDO: *The great philosopher Immanuel Kant says that it is wrong to treat people simply as a means to an end. If we're not concerned about* our feelings going into the future, then we're treating each other purely as tools for the gratification of our sexual desires. The point is that drink undermines our ability to make a judgement about how we really feel about a sexual encounter.

AENEAS: But all kinds of things undermine our ability to make that judgement. Maybe we're lonely, or we haven't had sex for a long time, or we feel unloved, or we're desperate for a meaningful relationship. Neither of us is incoherent or unconscious. If people don't have sex simply because they can't be sure they won't regret it in the morning, then not many people are going to be having sex…

DIDO: Look we haven't brought any Trojans with us anyway! Now be quiet, and eat another date…

Is Dido right to suggest that people shouldn't have sex when they've been drinking — even if it is only a small amount — since they can't be sure that their consent is genuine rather than alcohol-fuelled?

RESPONSE ON PAGE 88

Quick Dilemma

You're a politician lobbying for the introduction of a law that will make it illegal for a man to have sex with a very drunk woman (as she cannot properly consent). However, you are wrestling with a conundrum that is making it hard for you to make the case for the new law. If a very drunk woman cannot consent to sex, then it isn't clear why a very drunk man could be expected to determine whether consent is real or not. If drink takes away the ability to consent, why does it not also take away the ability to determine whether consent has been given? And if so, why should the burden of sobriety, and thereby ensuring 'real' consent, fall only on the man?

Quick Dilemma

Noel Pomski is a lawyer currently fighting an unusual court case. Archaeological excavations have unearthed some extraordinarily valuable artifacts. His client is the only known surviving descendant of the original owners of the artifacts, and she is claiming that by rights they belong to her. The trouble is, Pomski can't quite figure out by which 'rights' this would be true: it just isn't clear to him that ownership rights should extend down multiple generations. After all, why should a person benefit simply because some distant, or not so distant, relative happened to be well off?

CAN I BRING POISON
ONTO A BUS?

Nancy Hazle has caused consternation among the passengers of the 6.50am Union Express bus service. She has got on board chained to a large box with the words 'Danger – Emits Poison!' printed on it. She explains that the box contains a slow-release poison, which will affect approximately five per cent of people exposed to it. The poison's range is indeterminate, but proximity will increase the chances that a person will be affected by it. The effects, though unpleasant, are rarely fatal, and while its victims might need a few days off work to recuperate, they'll soon be right as rain.

Her fellow passengers are not enormously pleased by this news. They indicate that it might be in her best interests to step off the bus immediately. But she objects that she needs to get to work since a lot of people depend on her, the bus is her only mode of transport, and she's chained to the box, so she can't leave it behind. Moreover, she insists that she is not behaving any differently to the way that they have all behaved on occasions, and that there is nothing immoral in her actions.

Is she right? Should Nancy be allowed to bring the poison box onto public transport?

RESPONSE ON PAGE 91

WHOSE BODY IS IT ANYWAY?

Thomas Jarvis wakes up after a night on the tiles to find himself in a rather unusual situation. There are doctors milling about his bed, to which, bizarrely, he is handcuffed, and he seems to be attached, via a panoply of wires and tubes, to a well-known professional footballer (and fashion icon), who is sitting on an adjacent bed, wearing a sarong, waving at him.

At first Thomas suspects alcohol poisoning, but then the doctors begin to talk to him. They explain that he has been kidnapped and chained to the bed by the footballer's official fan club. It turns out that the footballer has a rare disease that if left untreated will eventually kill him. The good news, though, is that Thomas has the power to save the footballer's life. It just requires that he stays lying on his bed for nine months, attached to the footballer, while his immune system purifies the footballer's blood (which apparently has been poisoned after the consumption of too much spice).

Thomas is not best pleased with this news. He objects that surely there must be somebody else who could perform this

function. He is told, however, that thorough checks of medical records have shown that only his blood is suitable for the task.

Thomas still doesn't think it sounds fair. But when he continues to complain, the doctors invite a wannabe philosopher, Bernie Scholtz, into the room, who explains that the footballer has a right to life, and that if Thomas insists on detaching himself from the wires and tubes, he will be condemning the man to death. Thomas doesn't have any great fondness for football, or sarongs, or wannabe philosophers, so he's not sure that this sounds too much like a bad idea, but he is perplexed.

Can it really be true that he is morally obliged to stay hooked up to the footballer for nine months just because the footballer will die if he does not?

RESPONSE ON PAGE 93

IS IT WRONG TO COMMIT SUICIDE?

Dorothy Shaeffer wants to kill herself. This is not a view that she has come to lightly. She has been thinking about suicide fairly systematically for the last five years – ever since she turned 40 in fact. She can think of reasons to live – her sister, for example, will miss her if she's gone – but she can think of many more reasons not to live. She would say that she is not depressed exactly. It is more that she is profoundly bored: she is suffering from seemingly terminal *ennui*.

Dorothy has thought hard about the morality of suicide. She knows that there are religious objections to the taking of one's own life. She is aware, for instance, that the Catechism of the Roman Catholic Church states that suicide is 'seriously contrary to justice, hope and charity'. But Dorothy isn't religious, and doesn't believe in the afterlife, so she isn't much impressed by such pronouncements. She has taken into account that some people, such as her sister, will mourn her death. But she does not believe that their suffering will be very great, and certainly not great enough to outweigh what she sees as her right to do as she wishes with her own life (including ending it). She is also aware that she might feel differently about things at some point in the future. However, she thinks that this is unlikely, and, in any case, she is not convinced of the relevance of this point: certainly, she does not think that she has any responsibility towards a purely hypothetical future version of herself.

She has canvassed other people's opinions about suicide, but so far she has heard nothing to persuade her that killing herself would be wrong. She is frequently told that she 'shouldn't give up', that 'things will get better', and that she 'should just hang on in there', but nobody has been entirely clear about why she should do these things. For her part, she can't really see that she stands to lose much of anything by ending her life now. She does not value it, and in any case, if she's dead, she's hardly going to regret missing out on whatever it is that might have happened to her had she lived.

Would it be wrong for Dorothy to commit suicide?
If so, why?

RESPONSE ON PAGE 96

Thought experiments to illuminate issues of personal responsibility, culpability and punishment

CRIME AND PUNISHMENT

Should We Spare The Guilty?
Should We Punish The Innocent?
Are You Morally Culpable Or Just Unlucky?
Is It Wrong For Evil People To Defend Themselves?
Is It Sometimes Right To Torture?
Can Worse Ever Be Judged Morally Better?
Was It Always Going To Happen?

Some of the most intractable problems in philosophy concern issues of moral responsibility, culpability and punishment. These issues are absolutely bound up in the debate about free will and determinism. If it turns out that people choose to do wrong, then it is easy enough to think that they are culpable for their crimes. However, if their choices are at least in part determined by factors beyond their control, then it is much harder to see how things such as free will and personal responsibility fit into the picture.

If whether or not a person commits a crime is largely a matter of luck, then perhaps criminals do not deserve to be punished. However, if we do not punish people at all, it's possible the effect would be to increase crime overall. This in turn might lead us to think that it is right to punish people even if they aren't responsible for their actions.

SHOULD WE SPARE THE GUILTY?

The Emperor Q. Woolius Liberalis has recently been suffering sleepless nights, troubled by an article he read in *Il Guardiano*. The article reported the discovery of a new breed of toothless lion and suggested that they would make excellent pets for Rome's more ailurophobic citizens. The Emperor saw immediately that they might be employed to a different end. Why not use toothless lions in the gladiatorial arena? As a good utilitarian, Woolius could see the justification for feeding criminals (and the occasional bishop) to the lions. There is a clear deterrent effect, and many people enjoy watching the spectacle of a giant Tibbles pursuing some poor miscreant.

The justification for this kind of thing is that it decreases crime overall, thereby contributing to the general happiness of the population. But these new toothless lions seem to alter the moral calculus. Why not simply pretend to execute criminals and bishops? A 'ferocious' attack by a toothless lion, a few blood capsules, a bit of acting and Bobius is your uncle – you get a deterrent effect, great entertainment and nobody dies.

Should the Emperor introduce the Lions With Added Safety Features (i.e. no teeth) into the arenas?

RESPONSE ON PAGE 99

SHOULD WE PUNISH THE INNOCENT?

Discontent is simmering in Chudleigh-by-the-Pond. An outbreak of robberies has deprived the village of many of its best oxen, threatening its chances at the county fair's annual 'Bovine Most Likely to Succeed' contest. Suspicion is rife, and a number of vigilante attacks have taken place in other villages.

The village detective, Inspector Horse, knows who is responsible for the thefts, but unfortunately the culprit has fled to South America. However, during his investigations, Horse has learned that Mr Campbell, the owner of a nearby soup factory, has previous convictions for stealing oxen. Although Campbell is not responsible for the current robberies, the Inspector knows that if he plants incriminating evidence at the factory, he will secure a conviction against him.

Inspector Horse briefly wrestles with his conscience, and then heads out to Mr Campbell's factory in order to create a trail of muddy hoof prints. He reasons as follows: The real perpetrator is out of reach. However, if Mr Campbell is arrested and imprisoned then the outbreak of vigilantism will end. The arrest is a good thing, therefore, since it promotes the greatest happiness of the greatest number of people. It is a straightforward utilitarian calculation.

Is Inspector Horse right to frame Mr Campbell?

RESPONSE ON PAGE 102

ARE YOU MORALLY CULPABLE OR JUST UNLUCKY?

David and John are enjoying curiously similar evenings. Both have spent the last few hours in their local pub drinking copious amounts of alcohol. Both have attempted to pull a girl, and failed. They have both strutted their stuff on a pool table, and got beaten. And both have explained to a bartender that their infidelity is really a sign that they love their wives. It's only as they leave the pub that their evenings diverge.

David and John get into their cars, and start to drive home.  Although they are both much too drunk to drive safely, they are not reckless in the way that they drive home. They keep to the speed limit, and take as much care as they can given their alcohol-impaired states. Halfway through their journeys, however, they are both involved in incidents.

David's Story
A child runs in front of his car. David brakes hard. Luckily, the boy notices the car, and manages to jump out of the way. David takes a deep breath, vows never to drink again, and drives, very slowly, and very carefully, back to his home.

John's Story

A child runs in front of his car. John brakes hard. Unluckily, the boy is listening to an iPod, so he doesn't hear the car, which hits him, leaving him badly injured. John is arrested for drink driving, and is now facing a stretch of time in prison.

On this particular evening, David and John have behaved identically. Both have spent some time in the pub, both have drunk too much, and both have driven under the influence of alcohol. The only difference is that in John's case the boy who ran in front of his car was wearing headphones, which meant he didn't hear the vehicle approaching, and therefore did not jump out of the way. But John is now facing time in prison, David is not.

Is John more blameworthy than David because he hit the boy? Or are both equally culpable for their behaviour?

RESPONSE ON PAGE 105

IS IT WRONG FOR EVIL PEOPLE TO DEFEND THEMSELVES?

'Free all Fluffies' (FAF) is a radical animal rights organization committed to ending the suffering of animals everywhere, particularly if they look cute. The members of FAF often employ extreme measures to accomplish their goals. The sight of a beagle gazing longingly at a pack of Benson & Hedges is enough to throw them all into a tizzy, and murder and mayhem will inevitably result.

For better or worse, after leaving a trail of death, destruction and homeless mink around the country, the members of FAF are now holed up in a compound in Tunbridge Wells, surrounded by armed police and a phalanx of angry turkey farmers.

THE FOLLOWING THINGS ARE ALL TRUE:

1. The members of FAF have committed terrible crimes in the name of animal rights (including murder, torture and kidnapping). In the world of this thought experiment, there is no doubt that they are evil.
2. There is no possibility that they can escape unnoticed from the compound.

3. If they are captured, they are certain to be executed.
4. The nature of the command structure of FAF, together with the psychological dynamics of the group and the inevitability of the execution of its members if they are captured, means that there can be no negotiated surrender. Inevitably the siege will end with a firefight between the authorities and the group.
5. There is a small percentage chance that any particular member of the organization can avoid death or capture, and thereby live to do evil another day, if they defend themselves when the authorities attempt to end the siege by force. There is no chance of their avoiding death if they do not defend themselves (most likely they'll die in a firefight, but if they do not, they'll be executed).

The question then is:

Is it wrong for any individual member of FAF to defend themselves in the event of an attempt by the authorities to end the siege by force?

RESPONSE ON PAGE 108

IS IT SOMETIMES RIGHT TO TORTURE?

Special Agent Zack Glower is in trouble. His colleague, Roger Dalton, doyen of an unfortunate pacifist tendency in the intelligence community, has messed up. He has allowed John 'Goldtooth' Bentham, evil genius and amateur philosopher, to plant a bomb that will destroy the whole world. Happily Goldtooth is in custody; unhappily he isn't talking.

ZACK GLOWER KNOWS FOR CERTAIN THAT THE FOLLOWING THINGS ARE TRUE:

1. The bomb will explode within the next 24 hours (isn't that always the way...).
2. It will kill everybody in the world if it explodes.
3. If bomb disposal experts get to the bomb before it explodes, there's a chance it could be diffused.
4. Goldtooth is an evil genius: therefore, he cannot be tricked into revealing the location of the bomb, nor is it possible to appeal to his better nature, nor is it possible to persuade him that he was wrong to plant the bomb in the first place (Dalton has already tried this tactic, and it didn't go well).
5. There is a chance that Goldtooth is not aware of the bomb's location.
6. If Goldtooth is tortured, then there is a chance that he will give up the bomb's location (assuming that he knows the location).

7. There is a chance, however, that Goldtooth will be tortured for nothing: either because he does not know the location of the bomb, or because he will not reveal it.

8. If Goldtooth does not reveal the location, the bomb will explode, and everybody will die: there is no other way of finding out where the bomb is located.

Is it right to torture Goldtooth in the hope that he reveals the location of the bomb?

RESPONSE ON PAGE III

CAN WORSE EVER BE JUDGED MORALLY BETTER?

Bill and Ben are identical twins, but they are unlike any other identical twins who have ever lived. Perhaps the strangest thing about them is that they have lived (until now, at least) identical lives. The other odd thing is that they have different amounts of testosterone floating around their bodies: Bill is awash with the stuff, whereas Ben struggles to rouse himself even under the severest provocation. The twins' characters are as follows:

BEN

- Not aggressive
- No violent impulses
- Owns a poodle
- Rarely loses control

BILL

- Aggressive by nature
- Struggles with violent impulses
- Owns a bulldog
- Often loses control

Unfortunately, after a violent altercation in a garden centre, which involved Bill beating up a flowerpot salesman whom Ben was holding down, the twins have managed to get themselves in trouble with the law.

To everyone's surprise, the judge presiding over their case sentences mild-mannered Ben to two years in jail and aggressive Bill to only one year, despite the fact that Bill's assault on the salesman was more violent than Ben's. The happy news for Ben is that you have the chance to reverse this decision. The only catch is that your verdict has to be founded on sound philosophical thinking.

Should Bill receive a lesser sentence than Ben?
If so, why?

RESPONSE ON PAGE 115

WAS IT ALWAYS
GOING TO HAPPEN?

A strange legal case is taking place in the courthouse of the town of Westworld. An android gunslinger, known as Bruce, is on trial for murder. It seems that he ran amok on a film set, and shot dead a number of actors, apparently for the transgression of unrestrained method acting. Normally when such events occur involving androids they end up in a repair shop, rather than court, but it turned out that there was nothing actually wrong with Bruce. He just didn't like actors. The authorities could hardly turn a blind eye to his rampage, so he ended up in the courthouse. He is currently being questioned by his own lawyer, who wants to argue that he isn't responsible for his actions, given that he's a machine, but Bruce isn't cooperating.

> BRUCE: *I want the court to note that I killed those Dustin Hoffman wannabes purely of my own volition.*
>
> LAWYER: *But Bruce, you are just a very sophisticated machine, are you not? You do not make choices. You are just electronics and software, both of which function according to mechanistic laws. There is no freedom here. You're basically a giant Meccano man, aren't you?!*
>
> BRUCE: *I have consciousness. I have feelings, desires, aims and intentions. I can make plans. I have projects. I'm capable of rational thought. This is the stuff of freedom. I wasn't compelled by any outside force to kill those actors. I was not malfunctioning. I was acting as I chose to act.*

LAWYER: *But all those things, all this consciousness, it's a function of your hardware and programming, is it not? There is no choice at that level: it's just cause and effect, rules and calculations. There's no room for free will there: you might think you are making choices, but the choices you make are determined by what's going on at the level of your hardware and programming.*

BRUCE: *Well that might be true, of course. But it is also true for human beings: you are no more free than I am. You are just sophisticated biological machines. The choices you make are a function of the way that your brain works, which is governed by the laws of biology, and ultimately the laws of physics. The only difference between androids and humans is that we are mechanical whereas you are biological. If humans are to be held criminally (and morally) responsible, then the same should be true of androids.*

Is Bruce right? Should androids be held criminally (and morally) responsible for their actions?

RESPONSE ON PAGE 118

How is moral reasoning affected by the fact that we live in a world of nation states and fellow citizens?

4

SOCIETY AND POLITICS

Are You A Closet Imperialist?
Should We Discriminate In Favour Of The Ugly?
Are We All Brainwashed?
Is Homosexuality Wrong Because It Is Unnatural?
Should Pornography Be Banned?
Are You Morally Responsible For Climate Change?
Is It Always Right To Resist Great Evil?

Some moral problems concern the actions of governments and groups of people rather than individuals. Consider, for example, the question of when it is right to go to war. An immediate thought is that defensive wars are justified, but wars of aggression are not. But suppose the government of a country is causing great harm to its own citizens. In that circumstance, are we justified in launching an attack against it, assuming that there is a good chance of victory? If not, then what about if we were able to bring down the government without launching an attack? What about if it were a democratically elected government – would that make a difference?

These kinds of questions, and others like them featured in this section, get to the heart of the issue of the proper extent of state power.

ARE YOU A CLOSET IMPERIALIST?

The country of Macoraba, located some way off the west coast of Scotland, is by most people's standards a little harsh in the way that it treats its non-conformists:

1. The punishment for engaging in sexual activity after the age of 30, which is banned on aesthetic grounds – quite reasonably, the Macorabans would say – is public flogging.
2. The penalty for excessive consumption of Fox's Party Ring biscuits is 60 days hard labour in an Asda Supermarket.
3. And if you're foolish enough to get caught watching an episode of *Celebrity Shepherd*, then you will be executed by firing squad.

Possibly this all sounds marvellously eccentric to non-Macorabans, and not too much to get worked up about. But for the non-conformists of Macoraba, the restrictions can have quite devastating consequences. It is true that Party Rings and *Celebrity Shepherd* are easy enough to resist, but it is a different matter when it comes to sexual activity. Although most Macorabans thoroughly approve of the law prohibiting sexual activity past the age of 30 and the way that its transgression is punished, a significant minority of over-30s are caught breaking the law every year, and as a result they are publically flogged.

This causes them enormous pain and distress, and sometimes results in death. The suffering caused by the punishment is extreme, and would be regarded by most other societies as an overly cruel and painful response to the offence.

For reasons not entirely clear, you have come into possession of a machine that will allow you to end this mode of punishment. Specifically, if you press a button, the machine will leave everything else exactly as it is except for the fact that people over 30 will no longer be flogged if they're caught having sex – they will be fined instead.

Do you press the button?

RESPONSE ON PAGE 121

SHOULD WE DISCRIMINATE IN FAVOUR OF THE UGLY?

The Society for the Promotion of Ugly People (SPUP) has launched a campaign to highlight the problems suffered by the aesthetically challenged. SPUP relies on evidence from the field of social psychology to make its case that ugly people are systematically discriminated against. The society points to research by social psychologists such as Karen Dion, Ellen Berscheid and Elaine Walster that shows that if you're plain looking, you're less likely than your more attractive fellows to be perceived as intelligent, pleasant, warm, well-adjusted, sexually proficient and competent. SPUP have sought to publicize this unwarranted stereotyping by means of a hard-hitting publicity campaign entitled 'Plain Speaking for Plain Folks'.

PLAIN SPEAKING FOR PLAIN FOLKS

Were you singled out as a troublemaker from your earliest days at Primary School?

Did you hand in first rate homework only to see your schoolmates get better grades than you did?

Have you been passed over for promotion in favour of the office dreamboat?

Do you find that people of the opposite sex tend not to respond well to you?

If so: IT'S POSSIBLE YOU'RE UGLY!

For support and further information, join SPUP, and fight to end discrimination against ugly people.

It is SPUP's view that societies should introduce legislation to ensure that their less attractive citizens get a fair crack of the whip. It points to the fact that not only do most people think that people with physical disabilities should not be discriminated against, but they also think that society should take positive steps to ensure that the disabled are able to play a full part in civic life. Similarly, there is a widespread view among groups advocating racial equality that it is necessary for society to discriminate positively in favour of certain racial groups in order to compensate for endemic racism. SPUP contends that the situation facing unattractive people is the same. They are discriminated against: therefore it is beholden upon legislators to introduce laws that will help to change this situation.

Is SPUP right that we should discriminate in favour of the ugly?

RESPONSE ON PAGE 124

ARE WE ALL
BRAINWASHED?

Richard and Dan live in a society that is thoroughly and harmoniously religious. Children are taught about God, sacred traditions, the importance of family and community, the truth of the Holy Scripture, but that's about it.

Richard and Dan, however, were brought up by their parents – members of the renegade Enquiries at the Periphery – to be secular humanists. As teenagers, they were closeted away, and put through an intense educational programme to teach them the overriding importance of science and scientific methodology. At first, they resisted, preferring the simplicity of their early beliefs, but under relentless pressure from teachers they inevitably they came to embrace a scientific worldview.

However, their education has not made them happy. They are alienated from the society in which they live. They know that their way of understanding the world is the right way, but they wish it were otherwise. They live lonely, miserable, friendless lives. They are considerably less happy than they would have been had they not been born to proselytizing secular humanist parents. They believe they were brainwashed as teenagers – that they were victims of a kind of abuse, which has left them unable to live as full members of their society.

Are Richard and Dan right to think they were brainwashed as children?

RESPONSE ON PAGE 127

Quick Dilemma

Susan Berg is dying. The drug that might save her life is very expensive, and it's only available in a single shop. Her husband, Carl, tries to borrow the money, but he only manages to get together about half of the drug's cost. He goes to the shopkeeper, explains that his wife is dying, and pleads with him to sell the drug for less money, or to allow him to pay the outstanding amount at a later date. The shopkeeper is sympathetic, but refuses, even though he would make a large profit on the sale. The husband is desperate, so he returns later that night, breaks into the shop, and steals the drug. Is he right to do so?

Quick Dilemma

You have led an unblemished life for the last 25 years: you're married, you have kids, and you're a church warden. However, when you were a teenager, you were involved in some petty crime. Your past catches up with you when the police come to arrest you for the crimes that you committed when you were young. The thing is you don't feel that you are now the same person as you were back then: it's as if they are talking about the indiscretions of a different person. If so, then there are fundamental implications for how we view punishment. How can it be right to lock anybody up for 25 years, when perhaps by the end of this time the wrong person is being punished?

IS HOMOSEXUALITY WRONG BECAUSE IT IS UNNATURAL?

Ted Kelp, pastor of the Eastboro Ecumenical Church, notorious for its slogan, 'God Hates Gays', has just been killed in an unfortunate accident involving a dog collar and a wayward placard. He is not surprised, of course, to find  himself at the gates of heaven; he is, however, rather taken aback to discover that God does not in fact hate gays, and indeed that some of God's best friends are gay.

This leads to a somewhat uncomfortable conversation with St Peter.

ST PETER: *I believe, Pastor Kelp, that you are on record as declaring that homosexuality is a perversion, contrary to nature, and an abomination. Now God doesn't take kindly to such talk, and frankly it's more than likely you're going to end up in the other place. But we are nothing if not fair up here, so how about explaining exactly what you meant when you said those things.*

KELP: *Well, obviously I believed that homosexuality was a violation of God's holy law. It seems now that this belief was somewhat wide of the mark, but I do want to insist that I had good reasons then to think that homosexuality was immoral. The key point is that it is unnatural. It involves behaviour that violates God's ordained natural order. Archbishop Akinola puts it this way:*
'I cannot think of how a man in his senses would be having a sexual relationship with another man. Even in the world of animals — dogs, cows, lions — we don't hear of such things.'

So when I said homosexuality was a perversion, I meant that it
was unnatural; that it was contrary to nature.

ST PETER: *Interesting. Marriage isn't found in nature. So would you say that*
marriage is a perversion?

KELP: *Ah, no. The point you're making is that there are some good*
things — candles, for example — that are not natural. Fine.
However, what is significant here is that while it is natural for a
man to lie down with a woman, it is contrary to his nature for
him to lie down with another man. It is this violative aspect of the
behaviour, rather than the mere fact that it is unnatural, that
makes homosexuality a moral wrong.

ST PETER: *Fascinating. But isn't it the case that it is in our nature to be*
tempted by things that shouldn't tempt us? Yet we certainly
believe it is right to deny that aspect of our nature. So it can't be
the case that something is morally wrong simply because it entails
acting in a way that is contrary to our nature.

KELP: *I'm going to hell, aren't I?*

Is Pastor Kelp right to think that homosexuality
is wrong because it is unnatural?

RESPONSE ON PAGE 129

SHOULD PORNOGRAPHY BE BANNED?

Two people – one conservative, one liberal – meet in a bar to debate the merits of pornography, and particularly the question of whether or not it should be legal. For the purposes of their discussion, they agree that pornography is sexually explicit images and texts that are intended to be arousing.

The conservative argues that pornography is immoral since it violates religious precepts that hold that sex is only to be enjoyed between a man and woman within the confines of marriage. Moreover, he argues that pornography will encourage forms of sexual behaviour – such as masturbation, promiscuousness, and various other kinds of non-procreative sexual activity – that are themselves intrinsically immoral.

He also adds that there are consequentialist considerations that suggest that pornography is wrong. In particular, it destabilizes marriage, families, and therefore society as a whole. More generally, it undermines the moral foundations of society, and as a result threatens social stability.

The conservative insists there are good grounds for making pornography illegal. It is right and proper that the state prevents people from engaging in activities that undermine the moral foundations of society and that transgress prevailing standards of morality and decency.

The liberal disagrees. She argues that there is a strong presumption that the state should not curtail individual freedom unless it is to prevent physical harm to others. It is certainly not its place to police the behaviour of individuals in order to ensure moral rectitude. There are no grounds, then, for preventing people from consuming pornography if this is what they want to do (however unwise their choice might be).

The liberal adds that this view is bolstered by three further considerations. The first has to do with free speech: pornographers have the right to seek out an audience for their products and to distribute them accordingly. The importance of free speech is such that it would require clear evidence that pornography causes substantial harm to justify censorship. This leads onto the second point, which is that there is in fact no such evidence: certainly no evidence to support the proposition that the consumption of pornography causes significant *direct* harm. The final point concerns privacy: given that there is no clear evidence that pornography is harmful, the state is not justified in interfering in the private lives of its citizens.

Who is right, the conservative or the liberal?
Should pornography be banned?

RESPONSE ON PAGE 132

ARE YOU MORALLY RESPONSIBLE
FOR CLIMATE CHANGE?

Frank Assisi, the CEO of the environmental pressure group
Chums of the Earth (COTE) has been kidnapped by a band
of desperado Emperor Penguins upset that his campaigning
on global warming is spoiling their enjoyment of taking cheap
flights and driving 4x4s. The penguins, having discovered that
their flippers are not ideally suited to the task of handling
weaponry, are keen to avoid a violent confrontation with
COTE; they hope to use rational argument to persuade Frank
that his organization has taken a wrong turn. To this end, they
have hired a philosopher King Penguin, Pingutotle the
Peripatetic, to debate the issue of climate change with Frank.

PINGUTOTLE: *Your organization is committed to the view that every one of
us contributes towards climate change, and therefore that we
are all morally responsible for the consequences. Is that right?*

FRANK: *Yes, Pingutotle. We all have our own personal carbon
footprint, which is the amount of greenhouse gas emissions
that we as individuals cause both directly and indirectly.
We know that such emissions contribute towards man- and
penguin-made global warming; and we know that global
warming will cause an impact on the environment in such a
way that it will cause suffering in the future. It follows,
therefore, that we are all morally responsible for this future
suffering, and that we should take steps to minimize it.*

PINGUTOTLE: *So what you're saying is that if I stop using under-flipper
deodorants and no longer fly to visit my cousins in Hawaii
then fewer people will suffer in the future?*

FRANK: *Well no, I'm saying that if we all take steps to minimize our contribution to the world's carbon footprint, then fewer people will suffer in the future.*

PINGUTOTLE: *That's interesting. Is my personal contribution to this carbon footprint great enough so that if it is subtracted from it there will be less global warming, and therefore less suffering in the future?*

FRANK: *No. The effect that any one individual has on global warming is miniscule. But if you multiply it by the world's population — more than 6 billion people — then you get a large effect.*

PINGUTOTLE: *So, in fact, if I carry on exactly as before, and continue to take flights, to drive my 4x4, and to have regular barbecues, I will not be causing any additional suffering in the future. By your own admission, the effect that any particular individual has on global warming is negligible, is it not?*

<Penguin audience erupts in rapturous applause>

Is Pingutotle right to suggest that no individual is personally responsible for any bad consequences that might occur because of global warming?

RESPONSE ON PAGE 135

IS IT ALWAYS RIGHT TO RESIST GREAT EVIL?

The people of the planet Arouet are living under the yoke of oppression of the evil Torquemadans. The Arouetians have been forced to abandon their traditional way of life in favour of a strict adherence to Torquemadan social, cultural and religious mores. Most Arouetians, in the face of overwhelming Torquemadan power, have accepted their subjugated status. However, an Arouetian resistance movement (the ARM) has recently emerged, and has launched a number of attacks against Torquemadan targets. Unfortunately, the Torquemadan response has been brutal, resulting in the deaths of thousands of innocent Arouetians.

This has led the ARM to rethink its strategy for opposing Torquemada, as Captain Denis d'Alembert, its commanding officer, explains here to the ARM's assembled rank and file:

CAPTAIN D'ALEMBERT'S ADDRESS

Noble Arouetians, for the past three moons we have been fighting the Torquemadan menace with courage and fortitude. However, though our struggle is just, the path to freedom is obscure. The successes we have gained against our oppressors have come at a terrible cost. Torquemadan reprisals have been brutal and extensive: many Arouetian lives have been lost and many homes destroyed.

The rationale for continuing our struggle is not clear. Although subjugation is an affront to the Arouetian spirit, and resistance is an inalienable right, it would be wrong to think that resistance is worth all possible costs. We must recognise that many innocent Arouetians will lose their lives if we continue with our fight. Such losses might be tolerable if there were a reasonable chance of victory, but there is not. The extent of Torquemadan power means that our triumphs will only ever be limited and symbolic: there is no chink in the Torquemadan armour through which we might achieve our freedom.

The right course of action is clear. We must lay down our arms, and seek an accommodation with the Torquemadans, at least until the balance of forces is in our favour. To resist when it will cost so many lives, and when it will achieve nothing, is a clear moral wrong. It is time, my fellow Arouetians, to disband our glorious, but ill-starred, Arouetian Resistance Movement.

Assuming that it is true that the ARM have no chance of defeating the Torquemadans, is Captain d'Alembert right that it would be a clear moral wrong to continue to fight against their oppressors?

RESPONSE ON PAGE 138

RESPONSES

WOULD YOU EAT YOUR CAT?

(see pages 12-13)

*The 'Yuk-Factor', and how it is implicated in
moral judgements and behaviour*

This is a version of an ethical dilemma that is beautifully satirized in an episode of *The Simpsons*. Homer buys a lobster with the intention of eating it, but then falls in love with it, names it Pinchy, and declares that it is now a member of the family. He decides to give Pinchy a hot bath, but inadvertently boils him alive. There follows a classic scene in which Homer, tears streaming down his cheeks, tucks into Pinchy with gusto, declaring him delicious at the same time as mourning his death.

The joke works because people don't tend to eat their pets. However, the interesting thing is that it is not clear that there is a moral problem with it. So, for example:

    A. Hector was not killed so that he could be eaten
    B. He was not harmed by being eaten
    C. Nobody else was harmed by his being eaten
    D. Cleo was comforted by her having eaten
       Hector – it seemed like a fitting tribute

It isn't obvious then that there is anything about eating your own pet that would make it wrong. However, studies by psychologists such as Jonathan Haidt show that most people do think it wrong, though they are not clear why.

The 'Yuk-Factor'
One possibility is the existence of a 'yuk-factor' that becomes implicated in the moral judgement. In other words, people

are revolted by the idea of eating a pet, so consequently they judge it to be wrong. According to neuroscientist Steve Pinker, the reason why people have strong emotional responses to things such as the idea of eating a pet and yet remain unable to explain or justify what they're feeling is that moral convictions are rooted in the evolutionary make-up of the mind rather than reason.

Although most philosophers would resist the idea that *proper* moral reasoning can be rooted in emotion, it does not follow that emotion has no place to play in morality. The philosopher Jonathan Glover, for example, has argued that many of the atrocities of the last century were possible precisely because people's moral emotions had been switched off.

The Trouble with Emotion
Nevertheless, there are good reasons to be suspicious of moral judgements that are rooted solely in the 'yuk-factor'. Steve Pinker, in *The Blank Slate*, puts it like this: 'The difference between a defensible moral position and an atavistic gut feeling is that with the former we can give *reasons* why our conviction is valid.' A particular worry is that if we make moral judgements on the basis of feelings of revulsion there is always the possibility that we'll condemn actions – and even people – with no good reason. For example, the untouchables in the Indian caste system were not allowed to touch people from the higher castes; they were seated away from everybody else at public occasions; they were not allowed to drink from the same wells;

and in some regions, even contact with the shadow of an untouchable person was seen as polluting. Such prohibitions might sit easily with a certain kind of raw emotion, but they are much harder to justify in the light of reason.

So what of Cleo and her cat? Are you willing to condemn her simply because you find the idea of eating a pet repulsive? If so, what are you going to say when somebody condemns you because you behave in ways that they find repulsive?

MORALITY ⊙ BAROMETER

If you think Cleo is wrong to eat Hector

It is likely:

You value intuition or feeling in coming to moral judgements;

You think that even entirely private behaviours can be morally wrong;

You do not believe that it is necessary to provide a rational justification for all moral judgements.

If you think Cleo is not wrong to eat Hector

It is likely:

You value reason, rather than intuition, in coming to moral judgements;

You think it is important to look at the consequences of an action in order to assess its morality;

You do not think that intuition or emotion are good bases upon which to make moral judgements.

IS IT ALWAYS OK TO LOOK AT YOUR OWN PHOTOS?

(see page 14)

To what extent can we assume that informed consent extends over time?

It is possible that you think there is nothing here that is obviously morally wrong. Venus was 18 when the photographs were taken, she said that Milo could keep them, the photographs are not pornographic, and he's not shown them to anybody else. However, this response sidesteps a lot of moral complexity, the most interesting part of which has to do with how consent is affected by the passage of time.

It's a Matter of Consent
A particular issue here is whether Venus's consent that Milo could possess the photographs into the future was *informed* consent. Did she properly understand what it was to which she was consenting? A relevant point here is that when she gave her consent it probably was not possible for her to imagine how she'd really feel if she were confronted by the reality of the 40-year-old Milo, a man she did not know, looking at the pictures of her naked. It at least seems possible that if the

middle-aged Milo had magically turned up when Venus was making her decision, then she would have decided that perhaps she'd rather the pictures were destroyed.

Many people will not be persuaded of the significance of this objection. After all, we consent to many things in the knowledge that we can't be absolutely sure how we'll feel about it all in the future, but this doesn't seem to make the consent any less binding.

The Problem with Consent

Obviously, there is merit in this rejoinder, but it is not the end of the story. Consider, for example, the following conversation between Milo, aged 19, and Venus, aged 18:

MILO: *I love you Honey Bunny, will I always be able to make love to you?*
VENUS: *Oh yes, Pumpkin. I love you too. I'll always be yours!*
MILO: *Even if I were 40, bald and fat?*
VENUS: *Even then!*
MILO: *Even if you are as you are now — young and beautiful?*
VENUS: *Yes, until the end of time, Pumpkin. With my body, I thee worship!*
MILO: *I worship you too, Honey Bunny!*

Fast forward 25 years, Milo remembers this conversation, hops into his time machine, and zooms back to when Venus was still only 18. He's in her bedroom, and she's fast asleep...

Given this scenario, very few people will think that she has consented to a sexual encounter with the older version of her boyfriend. Yet the situation here is not so very different to the situation with the photographs. Even if she had meant at the time that she'd be happy for the older version of Milo to have sex with her, most of us would still say that the older version of Milo cannot assume consent. Quite simply, Venus did not really know to what she was consenting, so it was not informed consent. If we make the same judgement about the photographs, then it means Milo is right at least to worry that there might be something immoral about him continuing to possess them.

MORALITY BAROMETER

If you think it is wrong for Milo to look at the photographs

It is likely:

You think that entirely private behaviours can be morally wrong;

You believe that an action can be wrong even if there are no consequences that are obviously harmful.

If you think it is not wrong for Milo to look the photographs

It is possible:

You think that in the absence of harm an action will very rarely, if ever, be wrong.

IS IT BETTER TO BE A SEXIST THAN A MISANTHROPE?

(see pages 16-17)

*The issue of the moral value of treating people equally
as opposed to treating them well*

How you assess Harold's misanthropy as against Lou's sexism
will be partly determined by whether you think it is more
important to treat people nicely or more important to treat
them equally. A moral problem with Lou's sexism is that it is
discriminatory. He views and treats women differently from
men simply because he is prejudiced against women.

Harold's misanthropy, in contrast, is not discriminatory.
He does not believe that men are superior to women, or
indeed that any one group of people is superior to another.
However, he does not like humankind, and as a result his
treatment of people is worse than Lou's. He might not
discriminate, but people are less happy after meeting Harold
than they are after meeting Lou.

If you're a strict utilitarian, perhaps you'll think that it is
fairly clear that Harold's kind of misanthropy is worse than
Lou's kind of sexism: Harold contributes more unhappiness
to the world than does Lou. However, there are a number of
complications here that are worth taking into account.

Act and Rule Utilitarianism

The first has to do with a distinction between what is called 'act
utilitarianism' and 'rule utilitarianism'. The former looks
at the effects of particular *acts* in determining rightness
and wrongness, whereas the latter looks at the effects
of following particular *rules*. A rule utilitarian might argue
that although specific instances of misanthropy can be every

bit as bad as specific instances of sexism, it is still the case that sexism is a greater moral wrong, since if sexist practices were legitimate guides to rules for action, the effect would be worse in terms of the balance between happiness and unhappiness. The discrimination associated with sexism might breed resentment and a sense of injustice in a way that misanthropy would not.

This response, however, is not entirely satisfactory. Partly because it is possible simply to deny that the world would be worse off if sexism, rather than misanthropy, was a guide to rules for action. But also because even if there were no good utilitarian arguments to support the view that sexism is worse than misanthropy – in other words, even if rule utilitarianism does not support this conclusion – we might still want to make this judgement. Here's why.

Racism Rather Than Sexism

Suppose Lou is a dyed-in-the-wool racist rather than an unreconstructed chauvinist: his prejudice is directed against black people instead of women. Everything else remains the same. Lou treats black people better than Harold treats black people; in fact, he treats everybody better than Harold treats anybody. But Lou is racist and discriminates; Harold is not racist, and does not. In this situation, most people will think that Lou's racism is a greater moral wrong than Harold's misanthropy, *even if* the consequences of Harold's misanthropy are worse in terms of overall human happiness.

The key point here is that if people do judge racism to be worse than misanthropy, regardless of consequences, then it is not clear why the same judgement should not also apply to sexism, and other kinds of prejudice. The moral repugnance of racism is not that it has bad consequences, although it might, but rather that it is unfair and unjust. Sexism is similarly unfair and unjust, so it is at least arguable that if we think that Lou's racism is worse than Harold's misanthropy, we should draw the same conclusion about his sexism.

MORALITY ◉ BAROMETER

If you think Harold's misanthropy is worse than Lou's sexism

It is likely:

You think that morality is determined by looking at the consequences of actions;

You are a utilitarian: what counts is the greatest happiness of the greatest number of people.

It is possible:

You are not as concerned about issues of equality and justice, except insofar as they contribute to human happiness.

If you think Lou's sexism is worse than Harold's misanthropy

It is likely:

You think that there is more to assessing the morality of behaviour than simply looking at how its consequences affect human happiness;

You are concerned about issues to do with equality, justice and fairness;

You think prejudice is wrong even if the behaviour it inspires does not lead to bad consequences.

ARE WE MORALLY OBLIGED TO END THE WORLD?
(see pages 18-19)

*Are there limits to the moral demand that we should seek
to reduce human suffering?*

Goldtooth's argument in favour of ending the world is not as easy to counter as one might think. The first thing to say is that a number of the more obvious objections are not going to work. For example, it's no good arguing that people will be terrified if they know they're about to die, that they'll regret not completing their projects, not saying goodbye to loved ones, and so on, because they're not going to know. Goldtooth's plan is to end the Earth in the blink of an eyelid: one second we'll all be here, the next second we won't. As a consequence, any moral objections that are rooted in the imperative to reduce suffering, distress and unhappiness are not going to work. Goldtooth's scheme might be dastardly, but if it is, it isn't because people are going to be miserable as a result of its implementation, since they are not.

It's Not All About Suffering
A more fruitful approach might be to argue that Goldtooth is wrong to focus solely on suffering. It is possible to accept that it is important to minimize suffering as far as possible, while also insisting that there is moral value in happiness or satisfaction or any of the positive human emotions and experiences. If we accept that this is the case, Goldtooth's plan is wrong since it will preclude human beings from experiencing these things.

However, this objection is not as strong as it might at first seem. It is true that if a person is alive it seems it would be wrong to deprive them of good experiences. However, it is much less clear that this is the case for people who are already dead or for people who do not (yet) exist. After all, most of us would balk at the idea that contraception is wrong simply because it functions to prevent the birth of human beings who would otherwise have gone on to live satisfying lives. Similarly, it seems unlikely that it is morally preferable that there are six billion human beings alive at the moment rather than, say, three billion.

The Importance of Self-Consciousness
There is, however, a version of this argument that might help Dalton to persuade Goldtooth of the error of his ways. It is possible that humans are the only rational, self-conscious beings in the universe. It is not particularly implausible to think that a universe with rational, self-conscious beings is better than one without them. If this is the case, then Goldtooth would be wrong to extinguish humanity since he risks extinguishing rationality and self-consciousness.

Impasse?
Unfortunately, even this argument doesn't clinch the deal. Goldtooth can simply accept this point, but claim that the moral calculus still comes out in favour of wiping out human life. Specifically, he can argue that the imperative to minimize

suffering will trump any thoughts about the moral value of rationality and self-consciousness. No doubt Dalton will not be persuaded by such a response, and he'll probably regret having given up his licence to kill. However, there is a difference between finding an argument frustrating, believing it cannot be true, and being able to show that it is in fact false.

MORALITY ◉ BAROMETER

If you think we should end the world now

It is likely:

You think that there is a moral obligation to reduce suffering;

You think that it is more important to reduce suffering than to increase happiness;

You do not think that we should seek to ensure that there is sentient life in the universe at any cost.

If you think we should not end the world now

It is possible:

You do not accept that on balance human life is characterized by suffering rather than happiness;

You think that there is a moral imperative to ensure that sentient life is preserved in the universe;

You do not believe that the possible destruction of humankind is a moral issue that can be determined by rational argument.

ARE WE REALLY SORRY THAT HITLER EXISTED?

(see pages 20-21)

*Is it morally required to regret the occurrence of
some large harm if one's own existence depends upon it?*

This is a version of a moral paradox discussed by philosopher
Saul Smilansky in his book *10 Moral Paradoxes*. Put simply, the
paradox is as follows:

1. It seems morally wrong not to regret that some
   large harm has occurred.
2. It seems at best morally problematic to regret
   one's own non-existence.

The paradox arises if these two things are brought together
so that a person's existence depends on the occurrence of some
large harm. In this situation, if they do not regret their own
existence, it seems that they *cannot* regret the occurrence of the
large harm (in the sense that they cannot be sorry that it
occurred). On the other hand, it would seem at the very least
odd if someone regretted their own existence *simply* because
something like the Holocaust occurred (in fact, it is hard to
imagine such a thing).

Paradox Dissolved?
The solution to this paradox is not obvious. Perhaps one
approach is to argue that there is in fact no moral
requirement to regret the occurrence of some large harm if
such regret is conditional upon our own non-existence. In
this sense, the dilemma is a retroactive version of this
well known conundrum.

> Would you sacrifice some X (your life, livelihood, etc),
> in order to prevent some harm Y (a murder, the
> Holocaust, a rape, etc)?

The point here is that if there is no moral requirement to sacrifice one's life in order to prevent a particular harm, then equally there can be no moral requirement to regret the occurrence of some harm if the only way it could have been prevented would have been at the cost of one's own existence.

However, although this dissolves one end of the paradox – the moral requirement to regret that some large harm has occurred – it still seems *strange* to say that one does not regret the Holocaust, for example. Is there a way of allowing regret back in again?

Regret Redux
It is only possible to gesture at how such an argument might be constructed. Consider, for example, the sorts of thing that one can say about a rape that has occurred, which resulted in one's own birth.

    A. I'm sorry that the cost of my existence was your rape.
    B. I'm sorry that you suffered.

The expression of regret can be about the brute facts of the situation. *I'm sorry it had to be that way. I choose existence, but if there were any way I could alter the circumstances of my birth, then I would.* This is an expression of regret: not that the rape occurred, but that it was the only way that one's existence was possible. This might not be enough, but it is not nothing.

MORALITY ⊘ BAROMETER

If you think you can be sorry that a large harm occurred	If you think you cannot be sorry that a large harm occurred
It is likely:	*It is likely:*
You do not think that expressions of regret are matters of logical consistency. In other words, you are willing to embrace the paradox, and assert that you do not regret your own existence, but at the same time you wish that the large harm, upon which your existence depends, had not occurred.	You simply accept the conclusion of the argument. You do not regret your existence; therefore, you cannot be sorry that the large harm, upon which your existence depends, occurred;
	You do not believe that there is a moral imperative to sacrifice your life in order to prevent some large harm.
It is possible:	*It is possible:*
You regret your existence; that, if possible, you would give up your life retroactively in order to prevent the large harm from occurring.	You think that there are other ways to demonstrate regret than the simple wish that the large harm had not occurred.

SHOULD WE SACRIFICE ONE TO SAVE FIVE?

(see page 22)

(see page 22)

How our moral intuitions can change even where it is not clear that there are good reasons for such a shift

This is a version of 'The Trolley Problem', first described by the philosopher Philippa Foot. Most people will respond that the driver should press the button to divert the train so that it only kills one person rather than five people. Certainly if you're committed to some version of utilitarian ethics, which states that the right action is that which maximizes general happiness, then it is very likely you'll think that the train driver is duty-bound to ensure that as few people die as possible.

Railway Bridge Variation

However, things begin to get interesting when you add some variation into the scenario. Imagine that you're standing on a railway bridge, and there's a very large man next to you. The only way to save the five people is to throw the man onto the track in front of the train, which will cause it to divert into the siding. Is this the right course of action to take? The calculation seems to be the same here as before: you save more lives if you throw the man onto the track. However, when people are 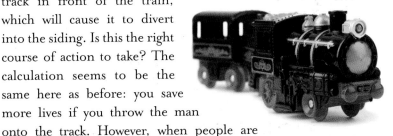 presented with this scenario, which was first suggested by Judith Jarvis Thompson, they tend to respond that it would be wrong to throw the man onto the track. In other words, they reject the course of action required by utilitarian ethics.

It isn't entirely clear why we have different intuitions about these two scenarios. Two factors seem to be involved. The first is that if the driver presses a button to change the direction of the locomotive, he is not doing something specifically to the man glued to the siding in the same way that we would be to the large man if we pushed him off the bridge. The second is that the man glued to the track is involved in what is unfolding, so his death does not seem quite as arbitrary. Neither of these explanations is wholly satisfactory, so our responses to this problem may have more to do with our psychology than strictly moral reasoning.

MORALITY ⊙ BAROMETER

If you think Pacey should press the button	If you think Pacey should not press the button
It is likely:	*It is likely:*
You think the morality of an action is determined, at least in part, by its consequences;	You think that consequences play only a minor part – if they play any part at all – in a moral calculus;
You think there is a moral obligation to reduce harm where possible.	You do not believe that there is a moral obligation to reduce harm.

SHOULD CLIMBING MOUNTAINS BE BANNED?

(see pages 26-27)

To what extent does the fact that we might unintentionally harm ourselves and other people curtail our right to freedom?

In one sense, it's a daft question to ask whether people should be banned from doing things simply because those things are dangerous. It just seems obviously a bad idea. Consider, for example: that it would require unreasonable restrictions on personal liberty; that life without any risk might be boring; and that momentous and worthwhile things – such as climbing mountains – can be accomplished even in the face of danger. However, what makes the question interesting is that we are not consistent in the way that we think about it.

Problems of Consistency

An obvious distinction to make here is between some activity being dangerous to oneself and it being dangerous to other people. Thus, for example, it might be thought that drink driving should be illegal because it is both dangerous to oneself and to other people; but that mountaineering should be legal because it is dangerous only to oneself. However, under close scrutiny this distinction begins to break down. Climbers, for example, especially inexperienced climbers, not only put their own lives at risk, but also the lives of other people – specifically, the members of rescue teams who have to pluck them off mountains. By putting their own lives at risk, they also run the risk of harming their loved ones if anything untoward should ever happen to them.

The British Home Office states that one of the purposes of laws outlawing certain drugs is 'to help protect people from harm'. If this is a good reason for legislating, then why not also make climbing mountains illegal? It cannot simply be a matter of assessing relative risk, since it seems likely that climbing a mountain is more dangerous, and risks more harm, both to the climber and to other people, than smoking a joint.

Traffic Terrors

A similar lack of consistency can be found in the way that we think about the motor car. In the United States, motor traffic accidents are the biggest cause of preventable deaths. Moreover, it is estimated that more than 20 million people have been killed in traffic accidents since the car was invented. The motor car also comes with huge social costs – to the environment, to our living spaces, and to the people whose lives have been wrecked by traffic accidents. Yet the motor car is legal, and cannabis, for example, is illegal.

Presumably the thought here is that this state of affairs can be justified by a utilitarian argument: the dangers associated with the motor car are compensated for by the benefits that it brings. The trouble is that it just isn't clear that this is true; moreover, there are other activities – such as smoking cannabis – where it seems equally, if not more, likely that this is true, and yet these activities are not permitted.

RESPONSES

A Libertarian Response

A possible way through these tricky issues is to take a libertarian view: that is, to argue that the state has no right to intervene in things such as drug taking or mountaineering, since these are fundamentally matters of personal choice. However, the problem with this view is that it simply ignores the fact that the number of truly private activities in modern societies is vanishingly small, and that there are potential social costs associated with any activity that impacts on other people. The central issue, then, is how we sort out the balance between individual liberty and social responsibility.

MORALITY BAROMETER

If you think that climbing mountains should be banned	If you do not think that climbing mountains should be banned
It is likely:	*It is likely:*
You think that the moral imperative to prevent harm is more important than any moral imperative to preserve individual liberty;	You think that there is a moral imperative to preserve individual liberty.
You think that the morality of an action is to be determined with reference to its consequences.	*It is possible:*
	You do not think that the state has any business interfering in the private actions of individuals.

SHOULD WE HAVE SEX WHEN DRUNK?

(see pages 28-29)

Can there ever exist such a thing as
fully informed consent?

It is necessary to get one thing straight right from the start here. Dido and Aeneas are not talking about a situation where a man or woman is so drunk that they cannot possibly consent to a sexual encounter. They are talking about a situation where both parties are able to reflect cogently on the issue of consent. Nevertheless, the worry remains: is it right to have sex with somebody if you know that it is possible they're only agreeing to the encounter because they have alcohol in their bloodstream?

The moral issue here is clear. The person you want to have sex with doesn't only exist in the present moment: what happens now will affect them in the future. Therefore, the fact that they want to have sex with you right now isn't the only thing you need to take into account. If you want to avoid treating them purely as a means for your own pleasure then you've got to worry about how they'll feel in the future about any sexual encounter.

Second-guessing the Future

The trouble is that this requirement disguises an awful lot of complexity. An immediate thought is that it simply isn't possible to know how somebody is going to feel about a sexual encounter in the future. Not least, it is possible that their life will change in entirely unpredictable ways to alter their feelings about it. However, this objection isn't as decisive as it might be supposed. Although it is not reasonable to ask somebody to refrain from sex because of the possibility that their sexual partner will come to regret the encounter, it *is* reasonable to ask them to refrain from it if they have *good reasons* to suppose that their partner might come to regret it. It follows, therefore, that if somebody is drunk, and you strongly suspect that this is the *only* reason they're consenting, you should not have sex with them, even if you both consider the consent to be genuine.

Moral Autonomy

The situation that Dido and Aeneas find themselves in is not quite this one, though. It isn't obvious that the only reason they're talking about the possibility of sex is because they've been drinking, and there is no particular reason to think that they'll regret the encounter in the morning – although this possibility is more than simply hypothetical. There are complicated issues here. Partly these have to do with treating people as autonomous moral subjects, capable of making their own decisions and mistakes. It is not obviously desirable that we should seek always to protect people from the consequences of their own decisions. Aeneas's point that there isn't really any such thing as consent abstracted from the messiness of everyday life is pertinent. Although alcohol might be a factor in any decision they make to have sex, there will be other factors too, and clearly

we cannot ask that people rid themselves of all extraneous influences before we allow their decisions to count.

There isn't an easy answer to this particular issue. It is perhaps a forlorn hope to think that people might always take into account the possibility that consent will come to be regretted, but this at the very least seems to be morally required.

MORALITY BAROMETER

If you think people should not have sex if they have been drinking	**If you think that people should have sex if they have been drinking**
It is likely:	*It is possible:*
You think sexual encounters should always be clearly and absolutely consensual;	You think that it is unrealistic to expect people always to refrain from sex if they have been drinking;
You think consent is necessarily undermined by the presence of alcohol in the bloodstream.	You think that consent, while necessary, is rarely untainted by external influences;
	You think that while alcohol has the potential to render consent meaningless, it is not the case that this occurs with the mere presence of alcohol in the bloodstream.

CAN I BRING POISON ONTO A BUS?

(see page 31)

*Is it always wrong to put other people at risk of harm
through our actions?*

Nancy's claim that we all regularly bring something like her
poison box onto public transport is actually correct: we do so
every time we get on a bus, train or plane with a heavy cold. We
know that we run the risk of infecting our fellow passengers,
we know that they'll suffer as a consequence, but many of us
will continue to use public transport when we're ill. It is clear
why it might be thought that such behaviour is wrong. The
philosopher J.S. Mill argued that every person has the right to
act as they want, *so long as their actions do not harm others*. If we get on
public transport while suffering from a heavy cold, then there
is at least the chance that we will harm some number of our
fellow passengers.

The Social Cost of Staying at Home

Happily, there are counter-arguments that suggest that it is *not*
wrong to travel while sick. Not least, there would be a
significant social cost if every time we caught a mild illness we
stayed at home, in terms of lost work hours and productivity,
and the effect on others who depend on our work. Also,
consider the effect on the leisure industry. Would we buy
theatre tickets if we knew that we couldn't go if we developed a
nasty sore throat? Would we book expensive airline tickets if
one sneeze meant that we would be barred from boarding?
Certainly it is likely that many people would not.

If there will be costs associated with us not doing things
simply because we have a (mild) infectious illness, then maybe

each time we get ill we ought to weigh up those costs against the benefits of us staying at home. If what counts here is some kind of personal cost-benefit analysis, then perhaps Nancy is quite right to think that she might be justified in getting onto the bus.

MORALITY BAROMETER

If you think Nancy should be allowed to get onto the bus	If you think Nancy should not be allowed to get onto the bus
It is possible:	*It is possible:*
You think that we do not have the right to insist that another person never does anything that might cause us (mild) harm.	You believe that freedom of action should be curtailed at least to the extent so as to proscribe actions that carry the possibility of causing even minimal harm to another person.

WHOSE BODY IS IT ANYWAY?

(see pages 32–33)

*Does the right of a foetus to life — if such a right exists — trump
the rights that a pregnant woman has over her own body?*

A version of this scenario was first posed by Judith Jarvis
Thomson in 1971 in her paper titled 'A Defence of Abortion'
to tell us something about the morality of terminations. The
debate surrounding abortion often centres on the question of
whether or not a foetus is a person, with all the rights –
including the right to life – that this entails. Thomson's
thought experiment challenges the
assumption that if the foetus is a person,
then abortion is going to be wrong. It asks
you to imagine yourself in a situation where
some other person's life is dependent on the
support provided by your body. Are you morally
required to continue to provide the support?

In Thomson's view, most people will find it
outrageous to suppose that there is such a moral
obligation: it might be an act of kindness to
continue to provide the support, but it is not
required. It follows, then, that it is possible to
grant that a person has a right to life, but to deny
that this entails the right to use another person's
body in order to stay alive. If this is correct, then
there are implications for how we see abortion.

Abortion

According to Thomson, a pregnant woman is
not morally obliged to carry a pregnancy to term,

since there is no moral requirement for her to allow the foetus to use her body in order to survive. If she chooses to abort, she does not violate the foetus's right to life, but rather deprives it of the sustenance provided by her body, over which it does not have a right. Abortion, then, is morally permissible (in certain cases, at least).

Arguments For and Against

Not surprisingly, this argument is highly contentious. Perhaps the most significant criticism is that the scenario outlined by Thomson is not analogous to the majority of pregnancies: whereas people normally choose to engage in sexual activity, and know that it might lead to pregnancy, the footballer's benefactor has been kidnapped. Arguably, this means that if a woman does become pregnant, then the foetus has rights against her that simply don't exist in the footballer scenario.

However, this objection is not decisive. Thomson asks us to imagine a situation where 'people-seeds' float around the air like pollen. You don't want them taking root in your house (since you don't want children), so you install mesh windows. Every so often, however, the mesh windows fail, and a people-seed will drift in and take root. Thomson argues that if this happens the person-plant does not have the *right* to use your house even though you voluntarily opened your windows. Likewise a foetus does not have the right to use a woman's body, even if she voluntarily engaged in sexual activity.

There are, of course, other criticisms of Thomson's thought experiment. For example, some people argue that there is a difference between letting a person die – as in the case of the footballer – and actively killing a person; others argue that by engaging in sexual intercourse a woman is tacitly consenting to a foetus using her body; and still others that in the situation described by Thomson there is the right to continue to use a body that is not one's own.

There is no general agreement about these and the other issues raised by Thomson's thought experiment. However, what is true is that she has shown how abortion might be defended even if one accepts that the foetus has a right to life.

MORALITY   BAROMETER

If you think Thomas Jarvis is morally obliged to help the footballer	If you do not think Thomas Jarvis is morally obliged to help the footballer
It is likely:	*It is likely:*
You think that the footballer's right to life is more important than Thomas's rights over his own body;	You think that Thomas's rights over his own body are more important than the footballer's right to life;
If you believe that the foetus is a person then you'll think that abortion is morally wrong.	If you believe that Thomas's situation is analogous to that of a pregnant woman, then you will not think abortion is morally wrong.

IS IT WRONG TO COMMIT SUICIDE?

(see pages 34-35)

Do the rights we have over our own bodies extend to the right to terminate our own life?

There are many arguments that aim to show that suicide is wrong; however, in this case at least, none of them is decisive.

A Utilitarian Argument Against Suicide

The most straightforward type of argument is a utilitarian one: Dorothy's suicide would be wrong because it would decrease rather than increase the sum total of human happiness. The attraction of this argument as it relates to suicide is obvious: if a person kills themselves, then the effect on loved ones may be devastating. The negation of the unhappiness of the dead person fails to compensate for the misery that their death introduces into the world.

However, there are problems with this argument. It isn't the case that it is always morally wrong to cause other people distress. Thus, for example, if Dorothy shops in Tesco, and her sister finds this terribly distressing, we would not tend to think that Dorothy is wrong to shop in Tesco because of this. More specifically, in Dorothy's case, it might just be that the negation of her unhappiness *will* in fact compensate for the misery caused to her loved ones by her suicide. As she stated, she does not expect that her death will be the cause of great suffering.

Misery Is Only Transitory

There is also a common thought that suicide is wrong because the misery that motivates it is only transitory. The idea here is that if the suicidal person waits long enough, then things will eventually get better, and they'll find that they come to value their life again. Suicide is wrong, then, because it deprives the person of good things in the future.

This argument also suffers from a number of weaknesses. In Dorothy's case – and in many real-life cases, especially those where chronic depression or illness is a factor – it just isn't clear that she will ever be in a situation where the positive in her life outweighs the negative. In other words, it isn't certain that she will ever come to value her life.

But even if she did have good reason to suppose that she will come to value her life again, it still isn't clear how this can be turned into an argument against suicide. It isn't obvious who it is that will be harmed if in fact she never comes to enjoy the good things that are in her future. It can't be the future Dorothy, since she will not ever exist to be harmed by having been deprived of these things; and it isn't the current Dorothy, since she doesn't value her life, and gains no solace in the idea of good things for a future Dorothy to experience.

Religious Argument Against Suicide
There are, of course, other arguments against suicide, but none of them is particularly persuasive. It is interesting here that even the religious argument that suicide is wrong because only God has rights over life and death doesn't stand up particularly well under scrutiny. The philosopher David

Hume, for example, pointed out that if suicide is a violation of God's rights, then so is saving the life of somebody who would otherwise face certain death.

Minimal Hope

Perhaps all we can do is to try to persuade Dorothy that she *will* come to value her life, and that this can be a source of comfort to her now. If this becomes morally relevant for her, she will have a reason not to commit suicide. Otherwise, it just doesn't seem that it would be wrong for her to end her own life.

MORALITY ⊙ BAROMETER

If you think it would be wrong for Dorothy to commit suicide	If you think it would not be wrong for Dorothy to commit suicide
It is likely:	*It is likely:*
You do not think that people have absolute rights over their lives and/or bodies;	You do not believe that there are good religious – or other deontological – arguments against suicide.
You do not think that consequential considerations of harm are the only factors in a moral calculus.	*It is possible:*
It is possible:	You think that an individual has absolute rights over their own life, including the right to end it.
You have religious objections to suicide.	

SHOULD WE SPARE THE GUILTY?
(see page 38)

*Are there reasons to punish a guilty person beyond
the effects of the punishment?*

Woolius Liberalis's dilemma arises from a certain kind of
utilitarian thinking about punishment. In its classic form,
originating in the work of the philosophers Jeremy Bentham
and J.S. Mill, utilitarianism holds that an act is morally right
to the extent that it has the effect of causing the greatest
happiness of the greatest number of people. In these terms, it
is right to punish an offender if the result is greater overall
happiness than would be the case if some alternative course of
action were pursued. The major benefit of punishment is that
it deters future crimes. If you know you're going to get fed to
lions if you steal your neighbour's ox, then you're likely to leave
the ox well alone. Crime is reduced and everybody's happy.

Deceiving the Public
The problem arises, however, because utilitarianism requires
the *maximization* of happiness, and it seems plausible that in
some circumstances this goal might best be served by appearing
to punish rather than by actually punishing. If one is confident
that an offence will not be repeated, and that the deception
will not be uncovered, it is not easy to see what will be gained
by making an offender suffer. Not punishing an offender
might sometimes be justified for purely utilitarian reasons.

There are, of course, problems with this line of reasoning.
It might be objected that it is simply not possible to fool people
about whether real punishment is taking place; and that even
if it were, that such a practice would be bound to become

public knowledge, thereby destroying the deterrent effect. However, such practical objections largely miss the point: as a matter of principle, people tend to think that horrific crimes should be punished, regardless of the precise utilitarian calculus. Most people will react with anger to the suggestion that a child murderer should receive only pretend punishment.

Retributive Justice

Retributive theories of punishment hold that justice is served if crimes are punished in proportion to the offence for which the punishment is a sanction. The central idea here is that the justification of punishment is that it is deserved. This idea has a long history. In Plato's *Republic*, for example, it is espoused by Polemarchus, who maintains that 'it is right to give every man his due', an idea that later appeared in Latin as *suum cuique tribuere* – to allocate to each his own. However, although it is easy enough to say that sometimes punishment is deserved, it is very difficult to explain why.

Imagine a world where punishment has no effects beyond the suffering it causes. It does not deter, rehabilitate, satisfy the grievances of the friends and relatives of victims, or contribute to the general wellbeing. Is it right to inflict harm upon a guilty person simply because he is guilty? There is no rule of logic against an affirmative response. However, it is difficult to see how it can be argued for, beyond asserting that it is a matter of moral intuition.

We are left then with a somewhat unsatisfactory outcome. If we take retributivism seriously, we will think that people ought to be subject to the punishments that they deserve and will balk at the idea that it might be right only to pretend to punish a guilty person. However, we may struggle to explain exactly what it means to say that punishment is deserved.

MORALITY ⊙ BAROMETER

If you think the Emperor should introduce toothless lions

It is likely:

You think that there is a moral imperative to avoid harm whenever possible;

You do not believe that punishment is justified simply because it redresses some harm.

If you do not think the Emperor should introduce toothless lions

It is possible:

You think that punishment must have a justification that goes beyond a consideration of its consequences;

You think that punishment is justified at least in part because it is deserved.

SHOULD WE PUNISH THE INNOCENT?

(see page 39)

*Is it ever right to victimize a person on the grounds that
it will benefit the greater good?*

Most people will find Inspector Horse's line of reasoning and
subsequent decision to frame Mr Campbell rather offensive.
It is surely wrong to arrest and punish a person known to be
innocent simply to secure some greater good. The
philosopher Immanuel Kant would certainly have thought so.
He argued that we should treat people 'never simply as a
means, but always at the same time as an end'. In other words,
we should not behave towards people as if their own wishes
and desires were of no significance. This is a general
complaint against utilitarianism: it can justify treating people
purely instrumentally.

The Case of Quarantine
There is, however, a lot to be said in favour of utilitarianism.
Consider, for example, that there are circumstances where we
tend to think it right to sacrifice people's lives in order to
benefit the majority. Quarantine is a good example of such a
set of circumstances. Most of us will accept that it might be
necessary on occasion to seal off a geographical area in order
to prevent the spread of a disease, even if it means that healthy
people within that area will fall ill and die. In such a situation,
we are in effect punishing a few people – the non-infected,
who subsequently become ill – in order to benefit the many.
Perhaps Inspector Horse has got it right after all – what counts
is the greatest happiness of the greatest number.

How About Torture?

This slightly disturbing thought leads to further similarly disturbing thoughts. Maybe it is OK to torture people if it serves the greater good? It is certainly possible to think of situations where this might be the case – a 'ticking bomb' scenario, for example, where there is only a limited amount of time to gain information that will save the lives of many people (*see* page 111). Alan M. Dershowitz, a Harvard law professor, has argued that in such a situation most people would expect law enforcement officers 'to engage in that time-tested technique for loosening tongues'.

No Easy Answer

We're in a bit of a mess then. It does not seem that Inspector Horse is right to frame an innocent man for the theft of the oxen in order to return Chudleigh-by-the-Pond to a peaceable state. However, the act of placing people into quarantine, even if it means condemning them to certain death, seems to be acceptable if it prevents a large outbreak of a deadly disease that might kill a greater number of people. As for torture – well, it's the kind of thing that people tend to find repugnant regardless of the justifications offered for it. But there is a question worth pondering here: Is it justified to torture an innocent person, if it prevents the torture of a thousand other innocent people?

If you think that torture can be justified in such a situation, then it is likely that your reasoning is solidly utilitarian, and perhaps you also have a sneaking admiration for Inspector Horse's policing techniques.

MORALITY ⊙ BAROMETER

If you think Inspector Horse is right to frame Mr Campbell	If you think Inspector Horse is wrong to frame Mr Campbell
It is likely:	*It is likely:*
You believe that the morality of an action is determined solely by reference to its effects;	You do not believe that the morality of an action can be determined solely by reference to its *immediate* effects;
You think that it is sometimes justified to harm even an innocent person if the consequence of doing so benefits the greater good;	You think that only on rare occasions, if ever, will harming an innocent person be justified solely on the grounds that it benefits the greater good.
You are committed to utilitarianism.	

ARE YOU MORALLY CULPABLE OR JUST UNLUCKY?

(see pages 40–41)

Does moral luck undermine our ability to make moral judgements?

The scenario here is set up to illustrate some issues involved in 'moral luck'. The phrase was first coined by the British philosopher Bernard Williams to describe those situations where a person is *correctly* judged in moral terms despite the fact that a large part of what they are judged for depends on factors outside their control.

Resultant Luck

The situation involving David and John is a version of moral luck that Thomas Nagel termed 'resultant luck'. Until the moment of the accident, David and John had behaved identically. However, because of a factor beyond their control – the presence, or not, of a set of headphones – their behaviour *resulted* in radically different outcomes. The significant point is that (without reflection) we will tend to judge them differently as a result, and see John as more blameworthy than David.

The account here is fictionalized, but it is easy enough to find real-world instances of resultant luck. Consider the case of Mahavira, the founder of the Jainist religion. At the start of his spiritual quest, he abandoned his wife, children and family. We tend to excuse his behaviour, since he founded a religion. However, suppose that for reasons beyond his control, Jainism had never emerged as a world religion. It is likely then that we would judge him much more harshly.

Are Our Moral Judgements Justified?

The key question is whether we are justified to make different moral judgements about people on the basis of factors that are beyond their control. This is a much more complex question than might be supposed. Perhaps a first thought is that it is entirely *unfair* that John is facing prison, and David is not. They have behaved in the same way, so they should face the same punishment. David's drink driving escaped police notice, but even had he been caught, he would not face John's penalty.

The trouble is the more one thinks about the issue the more complicated it becomes. Do we want to treat all drink drivers as potential child killers? Perhaps we do: but then does this mean we're going to imprison all drink drivers? If imprisonment is the appropriate punishment for people who have killed a child while driving under the influence of alcohol, it would seem to follow that it is also the appropriate punishment simply for driving while under the influence of alcohol (since you risk causing an accident involving a child).

It Gets More Complicated

Imagine two groups of people, Group A and Group B, where the people in Group A regularly drink drive, and the people in Group B do not. It turns out that the only difference between the two groups is that the people in Group A are genetically predisposed towards alcoholism. If the people in Group B had the alcoholism gene, they too would drink drive. This is an example of moral luck. Group A will be judged differently than Group B purely because of a factor – in this case, a genetic factor – that is outside their control. It seems to follow, then, that if we think that David is no less guilty than John for his drink driving (since it is only good luck that David didn't hit the boy), we must also conclude that the people in Group A – who drink drive – are *no more* culpable than the people in Group B, who do not (since it is only *bad luck* that Group A people drink drive). This, of course, is highly counterintuitive.

MORALITY 🧭 BAROMETER

If you think John is more blameworthy than David

It is likely:

You think that the morality of an action is at least partly determined by its consequences, even if luck plays a part in those consequences.

It is possible:

You think that luck will inevitably form part of the background of any moral judgement.

If you think David is just as blameworthy as John

It is likely:

You think that judgements of culpability should not be affected by factors outside of the control of the person being judged.

It is possible:

You think that David and John are culpable for their drink driving, rather than (in the case of John), the death of the boy.

IS IT WRONG FOR EVIL PEOPLE TO DEFEND THEMSELVES?

(see pages 42–43)

*Is it ever morally wrong for a person to try
to save their own life?*

The conundrum that this scenario throws up centres on the question of whether it is wrong for an evil person to defend his own life if the consequence will be that he'll harm some number of innocent people in the process and go on to commit further acts of evil. There are two conflicting moral intuitions at work here:

A. It is not wrong to defend one's own life.
B. It is wrong for an evil person to take steps that might prolong their evil-doing.

The 'tough' response is to argue that in the situation described there is a moral obligation on the part of members of FAF to forego the chance of escape, and thereby to condemn themselves to death. It simply must be wrong for them to try to save their own lives given that the consequence will be harm to innocent people.

However, though it is easy enough to agree that the *admirable* course of action would be for FAF members to sacrifice their own lives, it is highly counterintuitive to think that there is an obligation to act in this way. Imagine, for example, that Hannibal Lecter has been bitten by a rattlesnake. Luckily, he has some antivenom, with which he can save his own life, but he will then go on to commit further acts of evil. It is not clear that Lecter is morally *obligated* to choose suffering and death over self-administering the antivenom – that he would be morally wrong to choose life when confronted by death.

Moral Qualms

However, the difficulty is that if one wants to argue that members of FAF are *not wrong* to attempt to save their own lives it is necessary to bite some pretty big bullets.

First, it requires one to at least countenance the possibility that it would be right for the authorities to launch an attack against FAF (if that is the only way to end the siege), but also that it would be legitimate for FAF to defend itself against the attack. This isn't quite a direct contradiction, but there is certainly a tension here.

A second point is that the notion that members of FAF are not wrong if they defend themselves flies in the face of a certain straightforward utilitarian calculus. If these people survive, they will go on to do further evil things. This will leave the world worse off than it would be if they had not lived. If you're an act utilitarian (*see* page 74), then it seems you're required to conclude that FAF members would be wrong to try to save their own lives. But, as we have seen, this is also counterintuitive.

The third point is that it seems implausible that evil people behave legitimately if they resist other people who are also behaving legitimately in wishing to terminate their evil. If a suicide bomber is about to detonate his bomb, we probably do not think that he has the right to use his explosives to kill the intelligence operative who is trying to prevent him from detonating his bomb, even if this is the only way he can save his own life.

There are no straightforward answers to this conundrum. It is possible that what's going on here is that our moral reflections are running straight into a brute fact about human psychology, namely, that *in extremis* most of us will try to save our own lives. If it just is the nature of human beings that they want to live, then, at least in a sense, the issue of whether this is right or wrong in any particular circumstance is redundant.

MORALITY ◉ BAROMETER

If you think it would be wrong for members of **FAF** to defend themselves	If you do not think it would be wrong for members of **FAF** to defend themselves
It is likely:	*It is likely:*
You think that if FAF members have a right to live it is trumped by a utilitarian calculus that shows that their evil is a negative presence in the world.	You think that it is asking too much to expect people not to defend themselves if their lives are under threat.
It is possible:	*It is possible:*
You think that FAF members have forfeited their right to life by virtue of their evil deeds.	You think that the right to life is non-negotiable.

IS IT SOMETIMES RIGHT TO TORTURE?

Does the 'ticking bomb' scenario undermine the moral case against torture?

This scenario is an example of what is known as the 'ticking bomb' justification of torture. The ticking bomb justification aims to show that in certain circumstances just about everybody will agree that it is right to torture a suspect. Thus, for example, the American lawyer Richard Posner has stated that 'if torture is the only means of obtaining the information necessary to prevent the detonation of a nuclear bomb in Times Square, torture should be used – and will be used – to obtain the information… no one who doubts that this is the case should be in a position of responsibility.'

The ticking bomb scenario provides a straightforwardly utilitarian justification of torture. There is some large harm that is about to occur. The only chance to stop that harm is to inflict some considerably smaller harm on somebody you think might be able to reveal information that will prevent the large harm. The risk that you will needlessly torture somebody who cannot or will not reveal the requisite information is counterbalanced by the chance that you will prevent the much larger harm. Therefore, it is sometimes right to torture.

Problems with the Ticking Bomb Justification

Although this is a compelling argument, it is not without its problems. Perhaps the most common strategy employed to undermine the argument is to question the assumptions that underlie it. Opponents of torture argue variously that:

A. It is rarely, if ever, likely to be certain that a potential torture subject knows the information that might be required to prevent a large harm from occurring.

B. Torture is an unreliable technique to extract such information – not least, people will say anything to avoid being tortured.

C. There are other more effective techniques than torture which can be employed to get people to divulge information.

D. If there is enough time to torture somebody to extract information then there is enough time to pursue other avenues to secure the same information.

E. Allowing torture on rare occasions will inevitably result in a slippery slope situation, where torture is routinely and arbitrarily used.

In Defence of the Ticking Bomb Justification

There is, of course, merit in these arguments, but they are not decisive. Perhaps the major problem is that the ticking bomb argument suggests that even if one accepts that these are all good reasons to avoid torturing someone, there are still occasions

where one might judge that it is the right thing to do. This is not as counterintuitive as it sounds. Put simply, if a situation is desperate, and there are huge numbers of lives at stake, and there are no other options, then it seems that we are as good as morally required to at least try using torture, if there's some chance – even if only a small chance – that it might work.

A Case By Case Scenario
The obvious rejoinder here is to claim that in the real world we'll never be in such a situation. However, this is to miss the point: once one allows that torture is not disallowed as a matter of principle, then it becomes acceptable to judge on a case by case basis whether it can be legitimately employed. Consider, for example, a situation where it is estimated that there is a 90 per cent chance that Person X knows the location of a bomb, which will, with 60 per cent certainty, kill half a million people on detonation; moreover, it is determined that there is a 45 per cent chance that Person X will reveal the location of the bomb under torture. If torture is not ruled out as a matter of principle, is it right to torture this person if it is estimated that there is only a 35 per cent chance that the location of the bomb will be revealed if torture is not

employed? It seems that it might well be the right thing to do: certainly one can imagine arguing that it would be right.

The issue of torture arouses strong opinions. However, if one accepts the validity of consequentialist moral reasoning then it is hard to see how one can say with any certainty that it is never right to torture a person.

MORALITY ⊙ BAROMETER

If you think it is right to torture Goldtooth	If you do not think it is right to torture Goldtooth
It is likely:	*It is likely:*
You think that the morality of an action is partly determined by its intended outcome – which in this instance is to avoid catastrophic suffering;	You think that there is more to morality than simply a concern with the consequences of actions;
You do not think that the use of torture is ruled out as a matter of principle.	You think that torture is wrong as a matter of principle.
	It is possible:
	You do not believe that ticking bomb scenarios accurately describe any possible real-world situation.

CAN WORSE EVER BE JUDGED MORALLY BETTER?

(see pages 46–47)

*Is there more to moral culpability than merely the seriousness
of the crime that has been committed?*

To get a sense of how one might think about this case, it is
worth considering exactly how the judge reached his decision.
We already know that Bill and Ben have lived identical lives. It
follows that the difference in their behaviour – Bill's greater
aggression – cannot have been produced by the lives that they
have lived. It must have been something to do with their
make-up. We know that they are identical in every respect,
except that Bill has more testosterone in his body than Ben.
We also know that testosterone causes aggressive behaviour.
Therefore, it follows that the cause of Bill's greater act of
violence is the testosterone in his body, something over which
he has no control.

Mitigating Factors

But why would the judge opt for a harsher sentence
for Ben? Testosterone might explain Bill's greater
aggression, but surely he deserves at least the same
punishment as Ben for the crime he has
committed? Obviously, this is a key question in
determining whether the original sentence was
correct. The important point here is that Bill
battles against his violent impulses: in this
instance, he attempted to behave well, whereas
Ben succumbed all too easily to impulses that
were not nearly as powerful. The judge has
reasoned that there was a moral value in Bill's

struggle against his natural tendency towards aggression, and that he should be rewarded for it.

It is possible that you now think that in a way this all seems quite reasonable. Maybe the judge got the original sentence right. It is certainly true that mitigating circumstances come into play when we make judgements about the wrongness of particular acts, and there does not seem to be any obvious reason why we should not include physiological factors amongst them.

A Slippery Slope

But, in fact, this way of thinking leads one into a series of seemingly intractable puzzles. On the one hand, it seems right that you cannot be responsible for what you do not choose. If you happen to be born with a predilection for murder and mayhem then it does not seem that you can reasonably be held to blame for that – it's just a fact about the world like any other fact. But, on the other hand, absolving people from responsibility for their physiological make-up and the impulses that flow from it might mean that we end up having to excuse the worst kind of predatory paedophile.

Choosing Right and Wrong

Perhaps it is simply that we expect people to exercise free will: to understand what is right and wrong and to behave accordingly? At first sight, this seems like a neat solution, and if it is, then we should hold Bill more responsible than Ben and reverse the sentence. But there is still a problem: it is undoubtedly the case that because of factors beyond their control, including aspects of their personality, people do things they would not have done otherwise. As the scorpion put it, when asked why he had stung the frog that was carrying him across the river: 'It's just what scorpions do.'

MORALITY ⊘ BAROMETER

If you think the judge was right to impose a lesser sentence on Bill

It is likely:

You do not think that culpability (or blame-worthiness) is determined solely by the extent to which an act is wrong;

You believe that culpability can be mitigated by those factors that are both beyond a person's control and causally related to a wrong act;

You think that aspects of personality can be such a factor.

If you think the judge was wrong to impose a lesser sentence on Bill

It is likely:

You believe that personality factors should only rarely, if ever, be considered to mitigate the seriousness of a crime;

You think that culpability is strongly linked to the extent to which an act is wrong.

WAS IT ALWAYS GOING TO HAPPEN?

(see pages 48–49)

*Is moral culpability undermined if there is
no freedom of choice?*

The issue that Bruce and his lawyer are dealing with here is the perennial one of free will and determinism. The lawyer is arguing that since Bruce's actions are thoroughly determined by his hardware and programming, he does not have free will. This matters because if he does not, then it is at least arguable that he is not morally responsible for his actions. Bruce's response is that while it might be true that his actions are determined by mechanistic processes, his choice to kill the actors nevertheless flowed quite clearly from his intentions and desires – it was not caused by a malfunction in his systems and it had not been coerced by an outside agency – and therefore it was freely chosen. The difference between the lawyer's take on the issue and Bruce's take is the difference between an 'incompatibilist' and 'compatibilist' view of free will and determinism.

Incompatibilism

Incompatibilist philosophers, such as Immanuel Kant, define free will in such a way that it is logically *incompatible* with determinism. Determinism asserts that every act is simply the effect of some prior cause (which itself will be the effect of a preceding cause, and so on). According to incompatibilists, a free action is one which is not an effect – it is rather, in technical language, 'originated' – but which is still under the control of the acting agent. If determinism is true, then this kind of free action does not exist.

Compatibilism

Compatibilist philosophers, such as David Hume, take a different view. They define free will in such a way that it is logically *compatible* with determinism. In their view, a free action is one which flows from the intentions and desires of the acting agent. If an agent is not in prison, does not have a gun held to their head, is not suffering from a mental illness, and so on, then they can be said to be acting freely. Free will by this definition is logically consistent with determinism. Determinism doesn't say that there are no actions that flow from the agent. It just says that there is *some* causal background that determines the action.

Why This Is Important

This is not merely an esoteric debate since it goes to the heart of what we take to be moral responsibility. If both determinism and incompatibilism are true – in other words, if Bruce's lawyer is right – then the whole notion of moral responsibility is under threat. If we do not choose our actions – and let's not forget that there are good reasons to suppose that we *are* just sophisticated biological machines – then it is not clear how we can be held responsible for them. If, on the other hand, compatibilism is true – if Bruce is right to think that what counts is whether acts flow directly from an agent's desires and

intentions – then even if determinism is true, we can hold onto some notion of moral responsibility. Specifically, a person, or android, remains morally responsible for their actions to the extent that they reflect their desires, intentions, personality and nature.

MORALITY BAROMETER

If you think androids should be held responsible for their actions	If you do not think androids should be held responsible for their actions
It is likely:	*It is likely:*
You think that free will and determinism are logically compatible;	You do not think that free will and determinism are logically compatible;
You think that an actor is morally responsible if their actions flow from their desires and intentions.	You think that an actor is only morally responsible if an action is not just some effect of a prior cause.
It is possible:	*It is possible:*
You think that human beings are just sophisticated biological machines.	You think that human beings are not just sophisticated biological machines.

ARE YOU A CLOSET IMPERIALIST?

(see pages 52–53)

*Do we have the right to interfere in the internal affairs
of other countries?*

This scenario is designed to shed light on the constellation of issues surrounding the concept of moral imperialism. This term refers to the impulse to impose moral values from one particular culture onto another culture (or cultures). Although the term 'imperialism' carries with it a lot of negative baggage, it is important not to prejudge the issue here: there might well be reasons to think that sometimes moral imperialism is required.

The Macoraba case illustrates this possibility. It features a barbaric punishment for an 'offence' that almost everybody in the West (and indeed elsewhere) would consider absurd. The question then is whether or not we are justified in ending flogging even if this is contrary to the Macorabans' wishes.

The Justifications for Imperialism

It is not easy to come up with a justification for pressing the button that will withstand rational scrutiny. Consider, for example, that a straightforward utilitarian argument will likely fail. While it is true that people suffer if they're flogged, it is also true that a good many Macorabans enjoy the spectacle of flogging – so the moral calculus will probably come out in favour of flogging. However, this does not mean that there is nothing further to be said in favour of intervention. The following example should help to make this clear.

Imagine that as a result of worries about what they call the dilution of their national character, the Macorabans begin to execute non-Macorabans. In this situation, it is likely that we'd choose to intervene even if we were unable to justify the intervention on utilitarian grounds, and even if we were unable to justify it at all beyond simply stating that it is morally wrong to murder people because of their nationality. Most people will embrace moral imperialism, even if the justification for doing so is not entirely clear, if it is the only way to prevent something that is perceived to be a great barbarity.

Human Rights
However, there is a fair amount of complexity here. Perhaps the most important point is that intervention will often be justified in terms of talk about the violation of human rights, particularly as legally codified in the Universal Declaration of Human Rights (UDHR). The problem here is that it isn't clear that you get a *moral* justification for intervention simply by referencing legal rights. To put it simply, the fact that the UDHR states, for example, that everybody has a right to life, liberty and security of person means little in moral terms unless such rights can be rationally justified. Unfortunately, as yet, nobody has shown how such a thing might be done.

The other point to make is that even if it is possible to justify a particular instance of moral imperialism, it is no less moral imperialism for that: the moral codes that provide justification are unlikely to be universal. In other words, while the intervention might be justified in terms of the moral standards of the intervening party, it is unlikely that everybody will accept the validity of those moral standards (and particularly not the people on the receiving end of the intervention).

Flogging Redux

None of this is to argue that it is wrong to press the button in order to end the Macoraban use of flogging as a punishment. It is to suggest rather that the moral justification for doing so is not clear. It is entirely possible, of course, that this is a result of the inadequacies of the way that we think about morality rather than the undesirability of intervention.

MORALITY BAROMETER

If you think it is right to press the button	If you do not think it is right to press the button
It is likely:	*It is likely:*
You believe that moral values are not relative to culture, and that flogging is a moral wrong;	You do not believe that we have the right to intervene in the affairs of other countries, even if this is in order to eradicate some moral wrong.
You believe it is justified to intervene in the internal affairs of other countries, if it is to the end of eradicating some great moral wrong.	*It is possible:*
	You think that there is no objective morality: right and wrong is defined solely in terms of the standards of particular cultures;
	In this particular instance, there is no moral justification for intervening in Macoraba, but you do not rule out intervention as a matter of principle.

SHOULD WE DISCRIMINATE IN FAVOUR OF THE UGLY?

(see pages 54–55)

What is the role of positive discrimination in society
and what are its proper limits?

The first thing to say is that the claim that we should discriminate in favour of ugly people – perhaps by introducing quotas for jobs, for example – is not as absurd as it might sound. The evidence cited that unattractive people are at a disadvantage is well established and persuasive. For instance, Irene Frieze and her colleagues discovered that attractive male MBA graduates, compared to their unattractive counterparts, commanded higher starting salaries and greater earning power over a ten-year period, and Chris Downs and Phillip Lyons found that judges tended to levy a much lower fine when dealing with an attractive person guilty of a misdemeanour than when dealing with a similarly guilty unattractive person. You only have to imagine how people would react were we talking here about members of a particular racial group to see that it is not obviously absurd to be worried about this kind of thing.

Is There Equivalence?

SPUP's view is that there is a moral obligation on the part of legislators to address the discrimination that ugly people face. This position gains credence from the fact that society has sought to address other types of discrimination. In the United Kingdom, for example, the 1995 Disability Discrimination Act made it unlawful to discriminate against people in respect of their disabilities in relation to employment and education (among other things). Similarly, the 1976 Race Relations Act made it unlawful to discriminate on the basis of race; and the Sex Discrimination Act of 1975 made it unlawful to discriminate on the grounds of sex. Discrimination because of disability, race and sex are real problems that warranted being addressed. But, as we have seen, there is plenty of evidence to suggest that the same is true of discrimination on the grounds of attractiveness. Yet there is no legislation...

A More General Worry?

There is a general worry here that we're just not consistent in how we treat different kinds of inequality. Consider, for example, how we tend to view intelligence. There is a lot of evidence to suggest that general intelligence is an inherited trait: we do not choose how much of it we have, and we're pretty much stuck with the amount with which we're born. Intelligence is strongly correlated with educational attainment, occupational success, income level, and other measures of success in modern societies. Having less of it puts you at a disadvantage. Yet we do not tend to think that this is something society should seek to alter.

Perhaps the thought here is that it is not discriminatory to reward intelligence since we can offer *rational* justifications for treating people differently according to their intelligence. However, the trouble is that rational justification doesn't seem to be a key issue when dealing with other kinds of inequality. Thus, for example, we can offer rational justifications for treating able-bodied people and disabled people differently, but tend to think that we should take steps to ensure they have the same opportunities as each other; and we cannot easily offer rational justifications for treating people differently according to their attractiveness, but it doesn't even occur to us that discrimination against ugly people might be worth addressing.

Not Practical

It will be objected that discriminating in favour of ugly people is not practical. However, in a sense, that's not the point. Even if it were practical, most people would not think that it was the right thing to do. The trouble is that when one considers the issue more closely, it isn't clear why it is such an absurd idea.

M O R A L I T Y ◉ B A R O M E T E R

If you think we should discriminate in favour of the ugly	If you do not think we should discriminate in favour of the ugly
It is likely:	*It is possible:*
You believe that unattractive people are subject to discrimination;	You do not believe that unattractive people are significantly discriminated against;
You believe that it isn't always right to treat people purely according to their merits (since discriminating in favour of ugly people means discriminating against the non-ugly);	You think people should always be treated simply according to their merits (ruling out positive discrimination);
You think the justification for positive discrimination is that it rectifies some already existing harm.	You do not believe it is practical to discriminate in favour of the ugly.

ARE WE ALL BRAINWASHED?

(see page 56)

Is it possible to be brainwashed into believing things that are true?

The notion of brainwashing usually carries with it the idea that a victim has been forced or pushed to believe various things that are palpably false or absurd. This scenario asks us to consider whether it is right to describe as brainwashing the inculcation of a worldview that many people think is rationally justified. Richard and Dan are committed to the truth of secular humanism, but they claim that they cannot help but think that way because of the nature of their upbringing and education. They have, in effect, been brainwashed.

What is Brainwashing?

A possible objection here is to insist that brainwashing involves employing specific psychological techniques – such as isolation and emotional manipulation – in order to ensure that people come to believe particular things. The trouble is that this definition seems to leave too much out. Scientist Richard Dawkins and philosopher Anthony Grayling, among others, argue that the *normal* religious education provided by churches, mosques and synagogues is 'brainwashing'.

Perhaps then what defines brainwashing is that it involves the passing on of beliefs that are presented as being *unquestionably* true. This allows in the teaching of religion as a kind of brainwashing, but also an awful lot else. For a large part of the 20th century, history was taught as facts and dates – no

questioning and nothing to suggest that the details of history are contested. Maybe this was a kind of brainwashing.

Maybe the only way to avoid the brainwashing charge is to cultivate a restless and questioning spirit in people through our educational practices. But here the case of Richard and Dan looms large again. They were both taught to be restless and questioning, and it is their claim that they have been damaged as a consequence.

MORALITY ◉ BAROMETER

If you think that Richard and Dan were brainwashed	If you do not think that Richard and Dan were brainwashed
It is likely:	*It is possible:*
You believe that our truth claims, beliefs and values are largely determined by processes of socialization and education, and that in this sense they are never freely chosen;	You believe that the concept of 'brainwashing' most accurately describes the process of employing specific psychological techniques in order to shape people's beliefs and values;
You think that the concept of 'brainwashing' is best understood as being independent of the content of any particular beliefs that have been inculcated.	You think that a restless, enquiring spirit, and a commitment to reason and evidence as the best to determine the truth about the world, is antithetical to the kinds of unquestioning belief inculcated by techniques of brainwashing.

IS HOMOSEXUALITY WRONG BECAUSE IT IS UNNATURAL?

(see pages 58–59)

*The Is-Ought gap, and its implications for
our moral judgements*

The argument that some behaviour is wrong because it is unnatural – or right because it is natural – is very common. It is unfortunate, then, that the argument doesn't work. Consider, for example:

- Climbing Mount Everest is wrong because it is not natural for human beings to exist at 29,000 feet above sea level.
- Vegetarianism is unnatural, therefore it is morally wrong.
- It is unnatural to abstain from sex, therefore Catholic priests are immoral (those that manage to abstain from sex).

The Is-Ought Gap

None of these arguments is in the least bit convincing. The reason has to do with what is called the Is-Ought gap, which was first noticed by the Scottish philosopher, David Hume. The Is-Ought gap refers to the fact that statements about what is the case do not imply further statements about what ought to be the case. Put simply, the fact that something in the world is a certain way tells us nothing about whether it ought to be that way. For example, if it turns out that humans are genetically predisposed towards violence, murder and mayhem, it would not follow that we *ought* to go around assaulting and killing people.

The Is-Ought gap means that Ted Kelp is going to find it very hard to make his case that homosexuality is morally wrong because it is unnatural.

Social Disruption

It is possible that Kelp could rescue a version of his thesis by turning it into a consequentialist argument. For example, he might argue that:

- Human beings are by nature heterosexual.
- Society is organized to reflect this fact.
- Homosexuality is therefore socially disruptive.
- This has bad consequences.

However, this argument is both empirically suspect and logically flawed. First off, it just isn't clear that homosexuality is 'unnatural': consider, for example, that homosexual behaviour is widespread in the animal kingdom (whatever Archbishop Akinola might think). Moreover, there is no convincing evidence to suggest that homosexuality is either 'socially disruptive' or that it is necessarily associated with bad consequences.

More significantly, even if it were the case that a consequentialist argument could be constructed against homosexuality, it would not follow that homosexuality was immoral. If there are bad effects of homosexual behaviour, then it is possible that these are a function of the way that society is organized. If this is the case, then it is quite plausible to argue that it is society, rather than gay people, that ought to change.

Not a Matter of Reason

It is entirely possible that Kelp's beliefs about homosexuality are not rooted in reason at all: they are just a matter of prejudice. If so, then moral reasoning is besides the point: it won't matter what conclusion a moral argument suggests, Kelp still won't like gays. It is this fact that makes him a bigot.

MORALITY ⊘ BAROMETER

If you think Pastor Kelp is right	If you think Pastor Kelp is wrong
It is likely:	*It is likely:*
You value intuition or feeling in coming to moral judgements;	You accept Hume's point that it is not possible to derive a moral ought from a statement about the way the world is.
You do not believe that it is necessary to provide a rational justification for all moral judgements;	*It is possible:*
You either do not understand, or do not accept, the Is-Ought gap.	You do not think that homosexuality is unnatural.

SHOULD PORNOGRAPHY BE BANNED?

(see pages 60–61)

*Anti-pornography feminism and the moral case
for and against prohibition*

It is likely that most people will have more sympathy with the views of the liberal than with those of the conservative. By modern standards, the idea that pornography subverts the moral fibre of society seems rather quaint. However, even if we are not convinced by the arguments of the conservative, we should not simply assume that the liberal is right. After all, it is entirely possible that there are other things to be said that might lead one to think that pornography should be proscribed.

Feminist Approaches

In recent years, the most important arguments in favour of censoring at least some pornography have been advanced by feminist thinkers such as Catharine MacKinnon and Andrea Dworkin. The general approach is indicated by the definition of pornography suggested by MacKinnon and Dworkin:

> We define pornography as the graphic sexually explicit subordination of women through pictures and words.

This makes pornography a subset of 'erotica', and reflects some feminists' belief that pornography forms part of the structure of domination of women. Thus MacKinnon and Dworkin identify pornographic material that presents women as dehumanized, as enjoying humiliation and pain and as

below
being depicted in positions of servility, as examples of the
kind of thing that will have the effect of subordinating women.

The Problems of the Feminist Approach

The importance of anti-pornography feminism is that it
shows how a case can be built against pornography on civil
rights grounds: to the extent that pornography subordinates
women, thereby violating their right to equality, it is not
implausible to suppose that women have rights against it.

However, one large difficulty here is that there is no
general consensus that 'pornography', however it is defined, *is*
implicated in the subordination of women. Thus, for
example, although MacKinnon claims that pornography
celebrates and promotes rape and battery, there are in fact
no studies that clearly show that pornography is a significant
causal factor in sexual violence (and there are studies that show
that there are other factors at work). Moreover, if one begins
to think about the different kinds of sexually explicit material,
then it is unclear how it might be determined whether any
particular words or image should be classed as 'pornographic'
in the MacKinnon and Dworkin sense.

No Consensus

This debate is still very much alive. It is
important to recognise that it is not only liberal
philosophers, such as Ronald Dworkin, who
reject the case for censoring pornography, but
also many feminists as well, who argue
variously: that pornography can act as a

counterpoint to traditional conceptions of femininity and female sexuality, that it can enhance and widen women's sexual experience, and that it isn't a good idea for feminism to line itself up with conservative evangelicals on the issue of sexuality.

How you view the ethics of pornography and its legal status will depend on where you stand on issues to do with free speech, civil rights, sexuality, state intervention, and so on.

MORALITY  BAROMETER

If you think pornography should be banned

It is likely:

You think that the state has the right to limit personal freedom in order to promote the common good (which might include equality between men and women).

It is possible:

You believe that pornography is intrinsically immoral;

You believe that pornography violates the rights of women by subordinating them.

If you do not think pornography should be banned

It is possible:

You do not think pornography has harmful consequences;

You do not believe that it subordinates women;

You think that even if pornography does cause harm, or is associated with the subordination of women, this does not justify the state legislating on the issue.

ARE YOU MORALLY RESPONSIBLE FOR CLIMATE CHANGE?
(see pages 62–63)

*The question of whether actions that have vanishingly small
bad effects can be morally wrong*

Pingutotle's argument here relies on what might be called the problem of tiny effects (or, more formally, what the philosopher James Garvey has called the problem of 'causal inefficacy'). If some large harm is caused by a vast number of people, then the contribution that any one particular individual makes to that harm is likely to be so small so as to be negligible (in other words, in the absence of that contribution, the world would appear to be the same). It follows that no *particular* individual is causing morally relevant harm, which in turn means there is no requirement to alter individual behaviour.

Collective Guilt
This is a very difficult argument to escape. One possibility is to invoke some kind of notion of collective guilt. So, for example, in the event that somebody was stoned to death by a large crowd of people, we would not be impressed if a particular member of the crowd had protested his innocence on the grounds that the stone he threw had not inflicted any great harm. We would tend to think that the fact that he was participating in the stoning at all was enough to make him morally culpable. However, the trouble here is that this scenario is not strictly analogous to the situation with climate change.

Guilty of What Exactly?
Partly there is a difference in terms of intent: taking part in a group stoning where the aim is to kill somebody is not the

same as unintentionally contributing to some future harm caused to as yet not existing people by participating in activities that in the present contribute positively to human happiness.

However, perhaps more significantly the two scenarios are different in the following way: the stone thrower, assuming his aim is true, does cause at least some harm to his target; the person who takes frequent flights and drives an 4x4 has no discernible impact on global warming, and therefore causes no discernible harm to the people in the future who suffer as a result of climate change. If there is no discernible harm attached to the activity, and no intent to cause harm, then it is much harder to see where the moral responsibility lies. So, for example, if in among the stone throwers there was somebody who threw a grain of sand, it isn't at all clear that we'd hold them to be culpable (certainly not in the same way as the stone throwers).

Virtue Ethics

It is possible that the best bet for constructing a response to Pingutotle is to turn away from consequentialism towards a virtue ethics approach. Consider, for example, the merit of the following idea: we compromise our virtue if we associate with things that have bad effects. Thus, for instance, we may cease to view pornography if we think that pornography exploits women, not because we think that by doing so we will ameliorate its bad effects, but rather because we would feel morally contaminated if we continued to view it. It is possible then that the reason we should desist from, or minimize, those of our activities that are associated with global warming is not that we will make the world a better place by doing so, but because we will compromise our virtue if we do not do so.

MORALITY 🧭 BAROMETER

If you think no individual is personally responsible for any bad consequences that might occur because of global warming	**If you think individuals are personally responsible for any bad consequences that might occur because of global warming**
It is likely:	*It is likely:*
You believe that the morality of an action is derived straightforwardly from its consequences;	You believe there is more to morality than simply assessing the direct consequences of a particular act.
You believe that climate change is not significantly affected by the choices any particular individual makes.	*It is possible:*
	You think that morality has to do with living the right kind of life, and that part of this means a concern for the environment.

IS IT ALWAYS RIGHT TO RESIST GREAT EVIL?

(see pages 64–65)

Is it always worth paying the price of standing up to oppression and tyranny?

The question of whether the Arouetian Resistance Movement should end its struggle against the evil Torquemadans juxtaposes a certain kind of consequentialist thinking with the idea that it is a moral duty to oppose evil. To put it simply, if you think that it is right to oppose evil, but also think that it is right to avoid actions that cause great harm, then if it turns out that opposing evil *will itself* cause great harm, you've got a moral dilemma.

Resistence Reprisals

There is no easy solution to this dilemma. Consider a real-world example. In June 1942, Reinhard Heydrich, one of the architects of the Holocaust, died of injuries sustained after an assassination attempt. In response, the Nazis completely destroyed the village of Lidice, now in the Czech Republic, murdering every single male villager over the age of 16, and sending the women and children of the village to concentration camps (where many of them subsequently died). In addition, more than 10,000 other people were arrested, imprisoned or killed. Heydrich's assassination was carried out by members of the Czech resistance. The moral question is this: if they had known in advance the likely consequences of the assassination would it have been right for them to have carried it out?

A fairly simple consequentialist response to this question is that it would not have been right unless there were good reasons to suppose that Heydrich's death would shorten the war, or in some other way reduce harm to an extent equal or greater than the suffering likely to be caused by any reprisals that followed.

More Complicated

However, this response is deficient in a number of ways. First, even on its own terms, it is suspect. Consider, for example, that one result of always giving way to an oppressor because of fears about the likely consequences of opposition will be the absence of any constraint at all on the way that the oppressor exercises its power. In other words, there are good consequentialist reasons for giving an oppressor at least some reason to pause before it acts even if the immediate result of doing so is an increase in suffering.

A second point is that there is a constellation of ideas to do with what it is to live a worthwhile human life that suggests that consequentialism isn't the whole story here. Mere existence – the fact of being alive – isn't the only thing we care about. It is not particularly counterintuitive to suppose that there are situations where people will choose to suffer and die rather than to tolerate a situation that they consider to be an affront to human dignity or that renders them less than fully human.

An Overwhelming Imperative?

A final consideration is that it is possible there are some forms of evil so depraved that resistance is a moral duty, if not regardless of the consequences, then certainly well beyond the point where any straightforward calculation of good and harm would suggest that there should be no resistance. The case of

Nazi Germany looms large here, but in the present day one might also consider the Taliban to fall into this category.

It is possible that Captain d'Alembert is right to think that the time has come for the ARM to lay down its arms. However, as his justification for this view relies on a consequentialist argument, we can say that he has not yet proved his case.

MORALITY ⊘ BAROMETER

If you think it would be a moral wrong for the ARM to continue to fight

It is likely:

You believe that the morality of an action is determined by its consequences;

You believe that if armed struggle is justified, it is only justified if there is a reasonable chance that it will achieve its goals.

If you do not think it would be a moral wrong for the ARM to continue to fight

It is likely:

You believe that there is valour in resisting great evil even if the consequences of doing so, when viewed in the light of a straightforward calculation of benefits and harms, suggest that resistance is not justified.

It is possible:

You think that there is a consequentialist justification for opposing great evil, which probably has to do with the long-term results of acquiescence.

FURTHER READING

GENERAL PHILOSOPHY
Blackburn, Simon *Think* (OUP, 1999)
Law, Stephen *The Philosophy Gym* (Headline, 2003)
Nagel, Thomas *Mortal Questions* (CUP, 1979)
Nagel, Thomas *What Does It All Mean?* (OUP, 1987)
Rauhut, Nils Ch. *The Big Questions* (Longman, 2005)
Warburton, Nigel *Philosophy: The Basics* (Routledge, 1992)

ETHICS
Baggini, Julian and Fosl, Peter *The Ethics Toolkit*
    (WileyBlackwell, 2007)
Blackburn, Simon *Being Good* (OUP, 2001)
Cahn, Steven *Exploring Ethics* (OUP, 2008)
Cohen, Martin *101 Ethical Dilemmas* (Routledge, 2003)
Rachels, James *The Elements of Moral Philosophy*
    (McGraw-Hill, 1992)
Singer, Peter *How Are We To Live?* (Prometheus Books, 1995)
Williams, Bernard *Morality: An Introduction to Ethics* (CUP, 1993)

THOUGHT EXPERIMENTS
Baggini, Julian *The Pig That Wants To Be Eaten*
    (Granta Books, 2005)
Cave, Peter *Can a Robot be Human?*
    (Oneworld Publications, 2007)
Cohen, Martin *Wittgenstein's Beetle* (WileyBlackwell, 2004)
Sorenson, Roy A. *Thought Experiments* (OUP, 1999)
Tittle, Peg *What If... Collected Thought Experiments in Philosophy*
    (Prentice Hall, 2004)

INDEX

PICTURE CREDITS
The publishers would like to thank the following for permission to reproduce images:
Cover images: Front cover: Dreamstime; back cover: iStockphoto
Alamy: p. 36; Getty Images: pp. 24, 70; iStockphoto: pp. 3, 4, 12, 13, 14, 16, 18, 21, 22, 26, 27, 29, 31, 32, 33, 35, 38, 40, 42, 45, 46, 47, 49, 50, 52, 53, 55, 58, 60, 62, 65, 66, 69, 71, 76, 80, 83, 86, 89, 91, 93, 97, 100, 103, 105, 108, 109, 110, 113, 116, 117, 119, 127, 130, 132, 136